DEBT
COLLECTION
MADE EASY

Debt Collection Made Easy
by Roy Hedges

Copyright 1999 Law Pack Publishing Limited

LAWPACK

10-16 Cole Street London SE1 4YH
www.lawpack.co.uk
All rights reserved.

ISBN 1 902646 42 8

Exclusion of Liability and Disclaimer

This publication is designed to provide accurate and authoritative information with regard to the subject matter covered. It is sold on the understanding that neither the publisher nor author is engaged in rendering legal, accounting, or other professional services. If legal advice or other expert assistance is required, the services of a competent professional should be sought.

Whilst every effort has been made to ensure that this Made Easy Guide provides accurate and expert guidance, it is impossible to predict all the circumstances in which it may be used. Accordingly, the publisher, author, distributor and retailer shall not be liable to any person or entity with respect to any loss or damage caused or alleged to be caused directly or indirectly by what is contained or left out of this Made Easy Guide.

Table of contents

Introduction - Debts are a fact of life

Most businesses, but especially the smaller ones, seem to accept late payment of the money owed to them as inevitable. Many don't even bother to start asking for their money until it is overdue. Contrary to popular belief, debt collecting is not about upsetting customers. In fact, if handled correctly, it will strengthen customer loyalty and increase sales. Additionally, if properly used, debt collecting could even become an important marketing tool.

Our government has recognised the problem of late payment and its effect on the economy. 'The Late Payment of Commercial Debt (Interest) Act' has been recently introduced, but unfortunately, it isn't working. Firms do not want to antagonise their customers. The general belief

note The problem of slowing cash flow grows more acute. Improbable as it sounds; this book will help you to make sure that your recalcitrant customers cough up.

is that demanding interest on an unpaid invoice will have a negative impact upon the very people they rely on to survive and grow. Running a business is difficult enough without having to wait 45, 60, 90 or even a 100 days for money that should have been paid within 30. There is a very fine line between hounding your customers for payment and not chasing them hard enough – so where does one draw it?

One solution to this vexing problem is to bring the collection process forward.

Remove those obstacles and excuses your customers use to delay paying you. Your customers will not only pay you earlier but they will also do so with a smile. Bringing customer service into your credit control function will release money needlessly tied up in your sales ledger - cash you can use to expand your business.

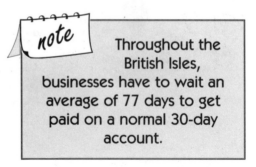

Throughout the British Isles, businesses have to wait an average of 77 days to get paid on a normal 30-day account.

In the majority of businesses, the sales ledger debt represents a sizeable asset, and therefore must be managed with the same diligence as any other valuable property. Remember, when you make a sale, all that you are doing is turning an item of stock into a debt. No profit is made until you have the cash in your bank account.

Understanding your debtors

1

Chapter 1

Understanding your debtors

What you'll find in this chapter:

➡ Why some customers don't pay

➡ Developing a collection policy

➡ What late payment can cost you

➡ Changing customers' payment habits

Companies both large and small suffer from the same headache - debt collection. Regrettably, it is the smaller firms, lacking the punch and self-assurance of their more established customers, who suffer the most. It is easier and certainly more cost effective to prevent debts from becoming overdue than to chase for late payment.

In order to carry through this objective, it is essential that you know your customers and understand how they operate their business. First of all, your collection process must be flexible. For example, it is no good chasing your customers for money on the 26th of the month if they always send their cheques out on the 25th! The same rule applies to invoices. Don't wait until the 25th or later to send an invoice if it is at all possible to ensure the invoice arrives in time to meet your customer's normal payment routine. This is one clear advantage a small firm has over its larger rivals. It can be adaptable.

> **TIP** The only person with an interest in getting paid on time is you. It is in your customer's interest to delay paying for as long as possible. The secret of successful debt collection is perseverance and a firm, but polite, approach.

Customer awareness is often neglected when it comes to collecting the money due to you. So take a leaf out of a salesman's book. Any good salesman or woman is aware of their customer's needs. They know which of their products the customer wants and which of those new lines will be of most interest. They will not waste time going through an extensive catalogue in the faint hope of an odd sale.

The same principle applies to debt collecting. Knowing before you pick up that telephone who does what and when within your customer's company will save you time and endless frustrating calls. Therefore, you must know exactly what happens to an invoice when it arrives at your customer's premises. To do this you'll need to acquaint yourself with the following details:

- the name of the person who books in your deliveries
- the bought or purchase ledger clerk who approves your invoice for payment
- who in the company signs and issues the cheque
- the name of the finance director
- telephone, fax, e-mail address and telephone extensions of the above
- account details (including the credit limit you granted) and cut-off dates
- what payments have been promised and when they are expected

This last item will allow you to forecast future cash flow more accurately.

It would also be helpful if details of your customer's payment history were available. Equipped with such information, you'll know that when they say they'll be paying you on the 28th, the cheque will definitely arrive. On the other hand, if they have a poor history of paying, you'll know to give them a gentle reminder a few days before the date agreed.

Cut-off dates were mentioned earlier; they will play a very important role in this process. Some firms pay for goods and services as soon as an invoice arrives while others wait to the very last moment before paying. Certain businesses, usually the larger ones, set aside a specific day each month to pay all their outstanding

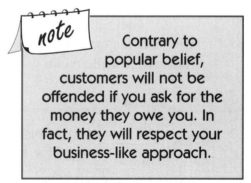

note

Contrary to popular belief, customers will not be offended if you ask for the money they owe you. In fact, they will respect your business-like approach.

bills. For instance, each of your customers probably has a regular cut-off date for invoices to be approved for payment. Now, if your invoice arrives the day after this occurred, it can't be included in that payment run, so you'll have to wait at least another 30 days before payment can be issued. Others stipulate the day upon which all cheques are issued and signed. Again, by asking for payment a day late, not only would you have wasted a phone call, but you'll also have effectively put back the date for receipt of the money with which you expected to pay your staff's wages. Can you afford to do this?

Knowing how your customer operates is good business practice. Being small and flexible allows you to use this practice to your advantage.

Getting the information you want from your customer needn't be a daunting task. Ask each new customer that requires credit account facilities to complete an 'Account Application Form'. This should become a routine feature of your business. The details given by the customer on this form will not only help you to assess the credit limit you will impose, but will

also provide you with all the knowledge required to speed up your collection process. For existing customers, simply ask them the next time you next speak to them about outstanding payments. It will show your customer you are interested in them and what they do, and that you care.

A combination of information gained through your new 'Account Application Form', the data relating to easier collections and the following information will enable you to set up accurate accounts:

note Having a historical record for each customer allows for continuity of your collection activity when you or staff is absent.

- the full name and address of customer
- value of the initial order
- name and address of bankers
- trading status of business
- at least two trade references

A copy of the customers' trading accounts should always accompany this form. Typical samples of both forms mentioned above come next. Reference to these forms will be made in Chapter 3, under Operating a Sales Ledger.

CUSTOMER HISTORY AND DIARY REPORT

Account No: _____ Credit limit: _____

Name: _____ Telephone No's: _____

Head Office Address: _____

_____

Fax number: _____

Invoice Address: _____

_____

Contact 1: _____ Ext: _____ Position: _____

Contact 2: _____ Ext: _____ Position: _____

Finance director: _____ Ext: _____

Sales manager: _____ Representative: _____

Area: _____

Cut-off dates: _____

Account Instructions: _____

Date	Contact	Notes	Follow up

Account No: _____ Continuation sheet. _____

Date   Contact   Notes   Follow up

_____

_____

_____

_____

_____

_____

_____

_____

_____

_____

_____

_____

_____

_____

_____

_____

_____

_____

NEW CUSTOMER ACCOUNT APPLICATION FORM

Name: _____

Address(Reg Off): _____

_____ Postcode: _____

Invoice address: _____

_____ Postcode: _____

Tel Number: _____ Fax number: _____

Comp/Man A/cs _____

Subsidiaries: _____

Man Dir/Prop: _____ Ext: _____

Fin Dir/Acct: _____ Ext: _____

Partners: _____ Ext: _____

_____ Ext: _____

Bought ledger supvr: _____ Ext: _____

Buyer: _____ Ext: _____

Account inst: _____

Bankers: _____

Trade Ref 1: _____

Trade Ref 2: _____

Annual Sales: _____ Credit limit req: _____

Audited a/c's   YES/NO   Branch codes: _____

Signed: _____ Position: _____ Date: _____

FOR INTERNAL USE

Date rec'd: _____ Salesman: _____

Initial Order   YES/NO   Rep's Report: _____

Ref's sent: _____ Date ref's rec'd: _____ Ref No: _____

Credit limit agreed: _____ Account No: _____

Credit controller: _____ Date: ____ Approved by: ___ Date: ___

Why some customers don't pay

One of the main reasons your customers do not pay on time is you, the supplier. Because, let's face it, you are the only one who has anything to gain by being paid on time.

 You can not simply sell and expect to be paid. You need that money to pay your workers, pay interest to the bank and pay your own suppliers. To ensure that there are sufficient resources in your bank account to meet your obligations, you must:

- ask for payment early rather than when it's overdue
- remove any obstacles your customer might have
- make your credit terms clear
- ask politely and often

If you're lax when it comes to asking for the money due to you, why should your customer bother? Suddenly, that nice customer you have been trading with becomes your debtor. Other possible explanations as to why it's to your customer's advantage to delay paying you as long as possible are:

- it helps their own cash flow shortages
- they can pay their suppliers early and obtain maximum discounts
- paying you late saves them paying interest
- your customers can use your money to expand

Thankfully, not all customers will be delinquent payers for the above reasons. Some may well have a genuine cause for their delay. It may be that goods are faulty, or maybe there is another legitimate reason for your customer to delay payment. If any of your customers have a problem with your goods or services, it is up to you to resolve the difficulty as soon as possible. See the next chapter for the easiest way to do this.

Developing a collection policy

You are in business to make a profit. However, until the money for goods or services you supplied sits safely in your bank account, you haven't any.

The collection of the money due to you must therefore be as habitual as opening the post each day. This advice applies to small businesses as well as large companies. It is vital to achieve full coverage of your customers when it comes to collecting debts.

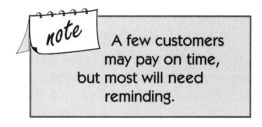

note A few customers may pay on time, but most will need reminding.

In putting together a collections policy, you must be flexible. A systematic approach is fine for your customers who pay on time or for those who need a gentle reminder. The hard core debtor, on the other hand, needs to be kept guessing by the fluctuation of your collection techniques. The severity of tone also needs to reflect the level of tolerance you will bear from those paying late.

The methods of accomplishing full collection coverage are:

TIP Any customer paying late is in breach of contract. You'd be guilty of this yourself, if you failed to deliver on time, so why accept it from them?

- A VISIT to the larger account customers in order to resolve disputes. This will build strong links with your customer, help you to avoid future problems and assist in the development of your marketing and sales.

- TELEPHONE as many customers as possible each month. Start with those customers who have the largest balances (not the greatest length of time a debt is overdue) and work your way down the list.

- LETTERS should be sent to all small accounts that are uneconomical to telephone. Letter cycles should be varied constantly both in the text and in their frequency for maximum outcome.

- FAXES communicate urgency. They can be used when letters are ignored and telephone calls aren't getting through. It is advisable to send faxes to the most senior managers for the utmost effect.

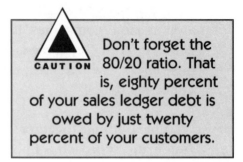

Don't forget the 80/20 ratio. That is, eighty percent of your sales ledger debt is owed by just twenty percent of your customers.

Put your collection policy in writing, for your own convenience and any staff you employ in the future. Set collection targets each month. Know exactly what amounts you can expect to receive and when. It's critical for your survival.

What late payment is costing you

Measuring the cost of overdue debt is simple. For the sake of this argument, let's say you're charged 9% per year for an overdraft. If you allow your customer 30 days' credit, every £1,000 sale will cost you £7.50 per month. Compare this to .75% monthly interest - it doesn't sound much, does it? Nor does adding a further £2.10 for inflation at 2.5% per year. Yet in the event a debt remains unpaid for six months, every £1,000 outstanding will cost you £57.60.

Assuming you are working on a 20% profit margin, the above sample would have eroded your profit margin by 29%. But interest rates and inflation are not always low. When they start to creep up again, the results could have devastating effect on your business.

Changing customers payment habits

Large organisations often have the audacity to presume their small business suppliers can wait for payment, but this type of attitude can actually bring harmful consequences to their liquidity. The introduction of CBI's prompt payment code and the British Institute's BS 7890, aimed at improving the payment practices in commerce, goes some way to solving this problem, but it will not stop bad debts from arising within the small firms sector.

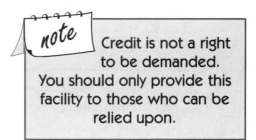

note

Credit is not a right to be demanded. You should only provide this facility to those who can be relied upon.

More businesses fail through lack of cash flow than any other reason, so it is vitally important to reverse any customer's bad habit of slow payment. Small business owners tend to shy away from chasing customers for payment, either because of old-fashioned British reserve, or due to the aversion of speaking about or asking for money. More simply, it is usually the fear of losing a valuable customer. Yet all is not lost! Later on you will be shown collecting methods to prevent late payment whilst retaining customer loyalty. By reversing this trend you will also find it is possible to:

note

- ensure you have sufficient cash to profitably operate your business
- regenerate cash tied up in your sales ledger
- save money on interest payments

TIP

Don't deliver goods to people who are perpetually paying late. If possible, use the non-delivery of your goods as a lever to get what you want from them.

- provide the money you need to expand
- improve customer service

What can you do to get customers to alter their payment methods? For a start, you can discuss your terms of payment openly. Be positive. Think of the money they owe your business as your salary. It could mean your survival.

Offering your customers discounts for early settlement is one method of inducing faster settlement of outstanding accounts. However, it can be argued offering discounts for early payment can offset the cost of granting credit. Discounts should only be used where a clear advantage can be identified by a vendor. To gain maximum effect, they should be used in conjunction with a sales drive aimed at attracting new customers. The main considerations for offering early payment discounts are:

- reducing finance costs
- eliminating cash flow problems
- promoting new sales

Introduce your collection policy in the early stages of establishing your business - and don't waver from it.

Unfortunately, there is one major problem allied to early settlement discounts. Here's what I mean: An inducement has been offered and taken by your customer, but even though this early settlement discount has been deducted from their payment, they still do not pay you on time! The dilemma you now face, especially when dealing with a big customer, is - do you chase for full payment and risk upsetting them in the process? Or do you let them get away with it, thereby dangerously increasing your costs? If you do decide to use early payment discounts, you must communicate to the customer your intentions in the event of late payment.

Generally speaking, this type of incentive to control sales and cash flow is best avoided, unless you have the confidence and strong controls in place to stop customers abusing the facility. There are better methods to use, as you will see demonstrated in later chapters.

Prosper from customers' disputes

2

Chapter 2

Prosper from customers' disputes

Putting into place a system that allows for customer complaints to be pre-empted, monitored and speedily resolved will not only reduce the number of complaints arising in the first instance, but will also improve customer relationships and your cash flow. What could a good disputes control system do for your business? It certainly should:

- let you know your customer has a problem and how that problem arose

- tell you the amount of money being retained due to a disputed invoice

- indicate how long it will take to resolve the problem

- ensure any money due to you is delayed for the shortest time possible

- ensure all problems are sorted out to a strict time scale

note

Having a simple system for monitoring customers' complaints is not only for large companies. Small firms can benefit too.

How customers' problems can delay your cash

When a customer complains, they either have a genuine grievance with your firm or are using the complaint as an excuse to delay payment, so it is important to learn as quickly as possible the ways to separate the real query from the excuse.

The reasoning behind the above statement lies in the fact that some customers with a complaint relating to your goods or service will refuse to pay what is owed until the problem has been resolved. A query over a comparatively tiny amount of money can hold up a very large payment. When you contact customers about an overdue payment, how often do you hear them say:

- Your salesman promised a discount of 2.5% and it wasn't shown on your invoice.

- I haven't received your invoice.

- Part of your order was missing - I'm waiting for replacements.

note

Trivial amounts waiting to be credited to the account, or small items waiting to be replaced,totalling perhaps ten or twenty pounds, could be holding up payments of hundreds, or perhaps thousands of pounds. The cost of replacing a dissatisfied customer is not easily measured in monetary terms. What they tell other customers or associates could have detrimental effects on your business in the long term.

Untying your money

Whenever a complaint surfaces, whether as a result of an alteration on a delivery note, or telephone call to or from your customer, you must acknowledge the dispute immediately. Keeping your customer informed as to the progress of their complaint indicates you care and value their trade. Such a response will not only show you are taking their problems seriously but will also tell them what you are doing to resolve the matter and how long you expect to take. An example of an acknowledgement postcard or fax message is given below.

You are more likely to achieve success if you treat your customers with this sort of basic respect. You might even get the customer to pay the invoice, less the amount disputed, and not hold back all the money due until the problem had been dealt with. Once this system has been operating a little while, your customer will have their confidence in you rewarded. They'll believe you will do what you say you'll do, in the time stated. If you manifest this sort of confidence, your customer relationships and your cash flow will both improve. This is turn might result in more orders. Conceivably, such a course of action might even lead your customers to recommend your firm to their friends and other business acquaintances.

D W COMPUTER SUPPLIES

To: <contact and customers name>

From:

Re: <customers order number or reference>

Date:

Dear

We are in receipt of your complaint relating to.................................. dated the XX/X/XX, and confirm this matter as been passed to the appropriate department with a request that the complaint in question is dealt with by the YY/Y/XX.

Should any further information be needed, please telephone or write to the undersigned stating our reference number C/...................

Yours sincerely,

MANAGER.

Proper use of the 'Customer History and Diary Report', as shown earlier, will help you to distinguish the genuine complaints from the customer's delaying excuses. After operating this system for a couple of months, you will have built up enough information to enable you to make solid observations about those non-payment excuses. Those customers who constantly request 'copy invoices', or who raise flimsy queries which on investigation are refuted will be identified. As soon as a pattern develops, tell your customer your findings. Tell them clearly and precisely what action you propose taking to avoid repetition of their behaviour in future. If necessary, only accept orders COD from those who repeatedly take unauthorised credit.

A simple system for resolving disputes

When setting up this system, you must first decide how long it should take to resolve a customer's complaint. In the majority of firms, five to seven working days is ample, but ten to fourteen days must be the absolute maximum period you allow. If you allow a customer's dispute to continue indefinitely, you only create problems for yourself. The longer it takes to deal with a problem, the less chance there is of an amicable settlement. These delays can be due to memories failing, staff who knew about the dispute leaving in the meantime and documents getting lost or misplaced. Not knowing if the complaint was genuine or not can result in the entire invoiced balance being written off unnecessarily. This means a loss of profits for you.

Keeping all your systems simple saves time, avoids errors and it won't 'clog up the works'.

Time spent resolving customers' queries is unprofitable. It doesn't require piles of paper being passed around from one department to another to resolve a query involving a few pence. The following three easy to understand forms are all that is required to operate a disputes system:

- a disputes form
- a disputes log
- a monthly disputes analysis

> **TIP** A good method for getting customer's complaints speedily resolved is the best debt-collecting tool you can have.

Your procedures can either be manual or computerised. For the majority of small and medium sized businesses, a manual system will be sufficient.

Don't over-look existing unresolved disputes. All customer complaints received prior to the start of your dispute register and are still unresolved must be inputted into the new system. Although a time consuming exercise, it will ensure no query will be overlooked in the transition stages.

A new or small business with only one or two employees may feel the following procedures are of no use to them. However time consuming it may seem, keeping a record of every dispute that 'Hits the Fan' is as important to you as it is to the multi-million pound conglomerate. You will see why as this book unfolds.

The dispute form

Ideally your form should be in two parts; the top will serve as a record of the nature of the complaint, the lower portion it's resolution. These forms can either be typed and photocopied, produced on a word processor, or better still, printed in pads of forms using carbonless paper with a perforated reply section at the bottom. For ease of handling and identification, the forms need to be in sets of 3 colours.

Whatever your design and content for these forms, they must be filled out promptly. Just as soon as a customer complains, or raises an account query, the person receiving the complaint should complete the top part of the form with the following details:

- customer's name
- the department or contact raising the query
- account number

- order number (if applicable)
- nature of query
- the action required to resolve the complaint
- the length of time available to resolve dispute

Do not forget to insert the invoice and account balances in their respective boxes. In the section marked copy documents, you will need to list copies of any supporting evidence relating to the dispute you're attaching to the form. Retain the top copy. All the other pages are then handed to the person maintaining your disputes system. Had the problem arisen in a credit department, the account ageing details would also have been inserted. If any other department had received the customer's query, the person responsible for keeping the disputes register would obtain this information.

Once the details had been entered into your system, the dispute would be given a reference number. One copy would have been kept on file and the remaining copies would be forwarded to the department concerned with resolving the problem. When that was done he or she would send an acknowledgement card to the customer. Importantly, this person would also inform your credit controller of the query, if you had one, who would then chase the customer only for partial payment, at least until the matter had been dealt with. All copies of this form should be retained in a ring binder for safety and ease of reference.

Let's say you agreed a discount of 5% with a customer and this was not reflected in their invoice. A credit note must be issued and sent by first class post. Should it not be possible to do this straight away, tell the customer at once what you have done and explain the delay. Once a customer's dispute has been satisfactory dealt with in this manner, tell the person responsible for your sales ledger so the disputed invoice is released back into the collection system and collected normally. The settled complaint can now be removed from the register, but not from your statistics.

DISPUTES FORM

Customer name: _____ Account Number: _____

Dispute type: _____

Invoice total: _____ Account total: _____

Complaint Number & Ref: _____

Aging: current   1 month   2 months   3-5 months   6 months +

Totals: _____

To: _____ Invoice number(s): _____ Order Number(s): _____

From: _____ Date: _____

Dispute details: _____

Instructions/actions required: _____

Completed by: _____ Date: _____

Copy documents attached: YES/NO

Tear off reply section

Reply:

Further action required:

Completed by: _____ Date: _____

Dispute classification

Having completed a dispute form by giving the form the next number available, the disputes controller would insert a disputes classification code or number in the relevant section on the form. This number identifies the type of query raised for analytical purposes. A list of usual customer's complaints you receive is to be itemised and a copy given to all concerned. For example, this would include:

- copy invoice requested - No 1
- VAT dispute - No 2
- short delivery - No 8
- goods returned - No 9
- sales query - No 14
- waiting service call - No 17

> *note*
> Send all large invoices by first class post, if they haven't been sent at the time of delivery. Generally speaking, the earlier a customer receives the invoice, the faster you'll be paid.

You will probably have many more types of dispute than those listed here, but then you'll be able to fill in the gaps between the above numbers more easily. Coding customer problems saves time and helps to cut down on the possibility of errors occurring. It also expedites the analysis and monthly reporting, making it much simpler for you to resolve your internal faults. This in turn will ensure you are paid on time in the future and your customers receive a much better service from you.

Disputes log

Prior to handing a disputes form to the person or department responsible for resolving the problem, details of the customer's dispute and how it occurred need to be recorded in a disputes log. This will log the date the complaint was received and resolved, customer identification, account value and value of the query, as well as the type of dispute being resolved. A suitable disputes log and analysis is shown below.

Summarising customers' queries

At the end of each month, together with your other management reports, you should produce a detailed breakdown of all the customers' disputes you have received and resolved. This monthly analysis will contain information you or your managers are required to know, such as:

- the total number of complaints received in the period

- the number settled and those still outstanding

- what types of problems your customers are experiencing

- a comparison of data to establish a trend of complaints and the action being taken to avoid reoccurrence in the future

The advantages of operating a simplified customer complaints system will not only speed the resolution of disputes and the payment of your invoices but also get you close to the market place. It should let you know what your customers want and how they react to your products or services. It will also pinpoint problem areas within your business and place you in a position to take remedial action to correct the faults that give rise to a customer's dispute in the first instance.

What you should learn from disputes

If complaints are quickly acknowledged and dealt with, not only will you see an improvement to your cash flow, but you could also see increased orders from your existing customers. You'll give added assurance to your customer if they know they can rely on you; additionally, you get the edge over your competitors. The careful analysis of complaints might also bring the suggestion of new products. Removing the root causes of customer queries helps to reduce the number of complaints in the future. It also reduces your costs, which in turn increases your profitability.

For example, suppose customers continually complain about late deliveries. Your complaints record will accordingly indicate a problem in your despatch or transport department. You might eliminate such a problem forever by simply appointing a new carrier or re-organising existing routes.

note It's not only the bigger firms who have complaining customers. Small ones do as well, but they can't afford to upset a buyer too often.

Chasing up unresolved disputes

Perhaps the account problem was not as simple as you first thought and it took longer to answer than you indicated to your customer. Having told your customer their complaint would be checked and rectified within five days, what should you do if after six days you are still waiting for your sales department to respond?

Of course, you will send the department concerned a reminder on the sixth day, allowing them two or three more days to deal with the problem. But what if there is still no response? A third reminder with a copy to the departmental manager or a director should do the trick. Whatever action you decide to take internally, don't forget to tell the customer what is happening to their dispute.

DISPUTE MEMO

To: <department resolving query>

From: Date:

Re: Outstanding customer disputes(s) No.

FIRST REMINDER

The attached copy dispute(s) remain unresolved, and have been outstanding in excess of 5 working days. Please ensure they are cleared immediately; alternatively inform me of the reason for the delay, and when you expect an answer to the problems raised.

Thank you,

DISPUTES CONTROLLER

URGENT

DISPUTES MEMO - SECOND REMINDER

To: <department resolving query>

From: Date:

Re: Outstanding customer disputes(s) No.

SECOND REMINDER - URGENT.

A FURTHER FIVE DAYS HAVE ELAPSED SINCE MY REMINDER MEMO DATED THE..............REGARDING THESE OUTSTANDING DISPUTES(S). IT IS IMPERATIVE YOU ATTEND TO THIS MATTER IMMEDIATELY.

COMPLAINTS CONTROLLER
copy to Sales Director.

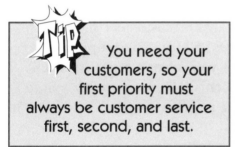

You need your customers, so your first priority must always be customer service first, second, and last.

So, you don't have departments. There is only you, a book-keeper, your partner and three or four other staff. Naturally you will not be sending out reminders, because you'll have assured yourself the problem was cleared up the next day, at the very latest!

Using customer service to expand

At every point of contact with a customer, your emphasis must always be on customer service. It is a practice carried out by salesmen and women all the time. So why not every member of your staff? Everyone should be polite when talking or meeting with a customer and friendly if possible - a smile goes a long way. Customers expect and deserve good service. A happy cheerful response with eye to eye contact will do more for your business than all the discounts and give away offers imaginable.

If you work for or run a large business, you might have a customer service department, in which case you may think a complaints system ought to be handled by them. If you let the customer service department resolve such complaints, make sure that they keep close contact with your credit controllers. Good communication between these two departments will ensure your customers aren't needlessly chased for payment in dispute.

A simple telephone call will go a long way in maintaining good customer relations. Take the time to explain any delay in resolving your customer's query, it's cause, and how long it will be before they can expect an answer. This is what keeps customers happy and loyal. Customers and their staff are only human; if you deal with their disputes promptly and keep to time schedules, they will know you can be relied upon. Your files will always be at the top of their pile, so your invoices should get paid first.

Avoid annoying customers and don't assume they're stupid. Listen to what they have to say carefully. Your business could rely on it.

Blatant lies are the sort of thing that angers customers more than anything else, so don't quote unrealistic estimates and try to push up the price later. Certainly do not entertain this practice if you seeking repeat business. Breaking promises and being late for appointments will never endear you to your customers. The two things customers hate most are:

1.   the 'it's nothing to do with me' attitude

2.   people who leave them waiting, or on the telephone, while conducting a personal conversation

Selling and collecting go hand in hand. It's a circle. When you are selling, your mind should be on collecting, and when collecting you should be thinking of the next sale. Every time someone from your firm contacts a customer, they should think sales. They should think collections.

Still saying you're too small for a disputes system?

Maybe you are a small firm with only a few employees, too small in fact to be departmentalised. In this case you can reduce the disputes methods explained to suit your own business. You may not require dispute forms, for example, but you should keep a record of when disputes arrive and when they are resolved. This is still essential information for any business to have. A categorised study of disputes, no matter how small, is indispensable to everyone in business. Especially those wishing to remain competitive and expand.

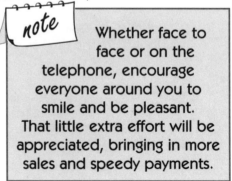

note Whether face to face or on the telephone, encourage everyone around you to smile and be pleasant. That little extra effort will be appreciated, bringing in more sales and speedy payments.

Sales ledger manage-ment

3

Chapter 3

Sales ledger management

A sales ledger is the most comprehensive record a business can have. Not only will it monitor the money owed to you, but it can also be useful for researching and investigating marketing trends for a new product or service or sales promotion.

A properly managed sales ledger can catalogue past product sales by region, thereby pinpointing the territories offering the greatest potential for your future sales initiative.

> **TIP** A well managed sales ledger can be a signpost to potential danger. It can also identify your good customers - those who always pay on time. That's the positive side of sales ledger management.

The sales ledger's role

Keeping itemised records of sales and payments received is not only a statistical record for accountancy purposes. It can also be a mine of information for customer appraisal and forecasting future cash flow trends. However, the basic task of your sales ledger is to chronicle the overall total and number of outstanding debtors at any specified point in time. These figures will represent a valuable asset in your balance sheet. Your sales ledger will also assist you in targeting outstanding sales income. Items displayed in a typical sales ledger would include invoices, cash, credit, and possibly debit notes. Care must always be taken to avoid mistakes, as your sales ledger needs to reflect a legitimate picture of what is owed to you and by whom. Your sales ledger debt is one of your few assets that can easily be turned into liquid funds, at reasonably short notice.

Individual accounts

Every new customer should be given an account number for easy identification and ease of access. Your customers' sales ledger accounts can be listed by any of the following categories:

- alphabetically
- chronologically
- by sales volume
- location

The first two options are normally preferred, with location and sales volume being the third and fourth choice. Once your business expands and you employ one or more credit controllers, the first two selections enable a fairer spread of customer mix. This is particularly important if customer visits are part of your credit controller's normal workload.

The key information to be recorded in your new sales ledger will more than likely be taken from the new 'Customer Account Application Form', but only after the contents have been verified. Whether you're operating a manual or computerised sales ledger, you should display the following at the top of the account page:

- the customer's account number
- customer's name and trading title (if applicable)
- address (both head office and/or invoice address if different)
- telephone and fax numbers
- name of contact and their position
- agreed credit limit

When numbering accounts, be sure not to miss or duplicate any numbers. In fact, this applies to all numbered documents; it is essential to be able to show a clear and consistent run of numbers for any government inspection.

The debit and credit entries of each account transaction should be written under the above details. An example of a typical sales ledger account, showing both brought forward and open-ended systems is displayed further ahead. The distinction between the two types of sales ledger systems mentioned is explained below. Whilst both are in current use, the open item method is more generally used because it has a number of advantages over the brought forward system.

The brought forward method

This method displays the outstanding balance of each account at the end of the previous month or accounting period. New sales are added as they arise and payments are deducted from the balance outstanding as they are received. The new account balance is carried forward when the current month ends.

BROUGHT FORWARD - SALES LEDGER ACCOUNT

Account No: _____   Credit limit: _____

Name: _____   Tel: _____   Fax: _____

Address: _____

_____

Contact: _____   Ext: _____

Salesman: _____

Date	Transaction	Merchandise	Vat	Cash	Balance
2.9.XX	B/fw				225.87
4.9.XX	Inv No. 0789	160.54	28.09		414.50
7.9.XX	Cash			414.50	
14.9.XX	Inv No. 0790	376.66	65.92		442.58
26.9.XX	Credit No. 059	12.60cr	2.20cr	14.80	427.78
30.9.XX	Bal c/fwd				427.78

The greatest disadvantage of this system manifests itself when the balance is brought forward. Unless transactions are in the same accounting period, it proves difficult to recognise individual invoices and reconcile them against payments received. Using this system can lead to errors in allocating cash if the full amount of the outstanding balance is not paid.

Open item system

DEFINITION

A sales ledger using the open-ended method displays each credit and debit transaction. This method allows easy matching of receipts against specific invoices, and allows overdue items to be spotted effortlessly. Generally speaking, fewer errors occur using this procedure. It stops you or your staff from wasting valuable time sorting out problems. This is especially true if the payments sent by your customer do not tally with specific invoices.

It is advisable to attach a perforated remittance advice to monthly statements for use by your customer. Anything you can do to help your customer to pay on time and help you to identify the payment when it is received must be beneficial. It is services like these that help to retain customer loyalty.

Most modern sales ledger software automatically matches the cash received against specific invoices, but the accounts will still need monitoring.

OPEN ITEM - SALES LEDGER ACCOUNT

Date	Transaction	Merchandise	Vat	Cash	Balance
3.9.XX	Inv No. 0789	144. 44	25. 28		169. 72
5.9.XX	Inv No. 0790	378. 24	66. 19		614. 15
2.9.XX	Credit No. 112	14. 68	2. 57		596. 90
25.9.XX	Inv No. 0791	73. 80	12. 92		683. 62
30.9.XX	Cash			169. 72	513. 90
2.10.XX	Inv No. 0792	34. 98	6. 12		555. 00

so forth and so forth....

Keeping accurate records is vital for staying in business. Therefore, you should ensure all invoices, receipts and credit notes are posted to the sales ledger daily. During the last recession, one of the major causes of business failure was the incapacity of firms to collect their outstanding debts. Cash and credit notes must be allocated to the items they clear. Payments posted to a ledger 'on account' need to be identified as soon as time allows. If there are queries concerning your customer's payment, telephone the customer, preferably on the day of receipt, to clarify the situation. Once the situation has been rectified and the payment has been allocated, confirm it in writing to avoid further mistakes.

TIP Instead of making notes on your sales ledger, use the customer history and diary reports. It's more professional.

Account queries raised by a customer relating to payment of an account must be dealt with promptly. The most effective way to handle customer complaints and to use their queries to your advantage was covered comprehensively in an earlier chapter. How to use this information when collecting will be shown in the next chapter. If you put all this advice into practice, it will most certainly help to reduce non-essential telephone calls and stress in the work place.

Talking to the right person at the right time will ensure you are paid on time each month. Your salesmen wouldn't approach your customer's accountant for an order, would they? No! They know who the buyer is and speak to him/her directly. So must you or your credit controller get through to the right person, the one who approves your invoices for payment or the person who signs and posts their cheques.

By correctly setting up your sales ledger account and properly recording customer details, you tell your customer that you:

- value all your customers
- intend to have a long and profitable relationship with them
- operate in a professional, business manner that they can rely on
- intend to be paid on time
- provide a high level of customer service

note Achieving these goals is only possible with accurate customer information. That means using the new customer account application forms, a business practice that can never be over-stressed. So far, only some of the advantages of using customer history and diary records have been shown. The time that they really come into their own is the time you start collecting your money.

Reducing the risk of bad debt

One of the tasks the sales ledger performs for you is the reduction of loss from bad debts. It is one thing to provide your customers with credit, but to do so without any idea you'll be paid back is reckless. No matter how carefully you vet new customers, you can only reduce the problem, never eliminate it.

Discerning which customers will pay you and which ones should be COD is easy. It is the large number of potential customers sitting between these two extremes that are the ones most difficult to recognise. If accurately assessed, however, they will be your main source of profitability.

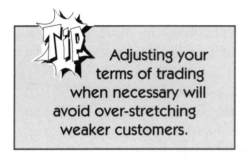

Adjusting your terms of trading when necessary will avoid over-stretching weaker customers.

This is where credit management comes into it's own, balancing the need for increasing sales while ensuring collection targets are met. At the same time, good credit management prevents late or non-payment. Whether you work alone or manage a large organisation, your risk assessment programme must be able to accept any promising and profitable order, to balance risk against profits and to decide the best time to commence collection procedures.

Start your customer vetting procedure just as soon as you are approached to supply goods or services to someone you have never traded with before. Prompt action will prevent any delay in processing the initial order. Your new account form has many uses; assessing credit risk is foremost amongst them. Remember that your priority in any credit search is to build a complete report of a potential customer's financial standing.

The amount of time spent on customer assessment will depend on the extent the customer wishes to trade with you. A small one-off order, or a series of fairly insignificant deliveries, will not warrant the same effort as a new customer requiring a substantial volume of regular orders. The main sources of information for assessing credit risk are:

- trade references
- credit reference agencies
- bank references
- customer's trading accounts

Trade references

Obviously, you'll ask your new customer to supply the names and addresses of at least two trade references. This is standard business practice. Your potential customer will not object to you requesting this information, unless they have something to hide. However, keep in mind that your customer is unlikely to give you the name of a trade reference unable to confirm a good trading pattern.

A customer must be asked to confirm the credit limit they expect to avoid any future confusion. A sample of a letter to a trade referee is given below. This request for information ought to be made as easy as possible for the recipient to deal with, so a stamped reply paid envelope is a must to ensure a prompt reply. Making these enquiries should confirm your desire to foster a sound business relationship between you both.

LETTER REQUESTING A TRADE REFERENCE

\<Company name\>
\<Street\>
\<Town & postcode\>

September 25.20XX

Dear Sir,

Re: D W COMPUTER SUPPLIES Your Acc No: YZ200234

The above firm has approached us requesting trade credit facilities and has given your company as a point of reference. We shall be grateful if you would kindly answer the questions listed below, on the enclosed copy letter. A stamped address envelope is enclosed for your convenience.

Please be assured of our confidential handling of your response. We shall be pleased to reciprocate at any time in the future.

Yours faithfully,

Proprietor

PLEASE INFORM US OF THE FOLLOWING:

1. How long has the above customer been known to you?

2. If a new account, were satisfactory references obtained?

3. What is your agreed credit limit with this customer?

4. On what terms do they operate with you?

5. Are payments prompt/sometimes late/always late?

6. Have you had to restrict deliveries at any time?

7. Is there any other relevant information you care to give?

The above information is given without responsibility of the signatory or company, and in the strictest confidence.

Signed: Position:

Date:

Credit reference agencies

In addition to trade references, it's advisable to obtain a credit agency search. One of the main advantages of using a credit reference agency is the speed with which they reply. They will also provide a comprehensive service. A few of these agencies names can be found in the section headed 'Sources of Credit Information'. Some of the information contained in the credit report from an agency may have been gained from other sources. This cross-referencing will do no harm; it should, in fact, strengthen your ultimate decision. The type of data you can expect in a report from a credit reference agency is:

- confirmation of customers name and address
- location of branches and nature of business
- amount of capital both authorised and issued
- list of subsidiaries or if part of a group
- turnover and summarised balance sheet details
- list of charges and/or county court judgements registered against the company
- recommendation of credit limits, and payment patterns with known suppliers

You may consider the information supplied by one of the larger reference agencies sufficient for your purposes, but it would be prudent to contact some, if not all, of the other sources mentioned. Only then can you be sure your decision to either withhold or grant credit, and the amount of limits you wish to imposed, is based on sound opinion.

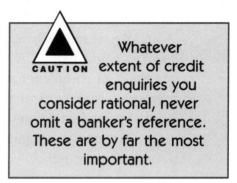

CAUTION Whatever extent of credit enquiries you consider rational, never omit a banker's reference. These are by far the most important.

Bank references

Bank reference are regarded as the best barometers for gauging a potential customer's worthiness, provided you understand the standard format of a bank's reply. The correct wording to use when requesting a reference from a bank and a translation of the bank's responses will be shown below.

Banks have a legal obligation of secrecy and confidentiality towards their client's affairs, which can prohibit disclosure of facts relating to the customers' accounts. When a bank receives a request for a reference, it assumes their customer has authorised them to give a report by releasing details of their bankers and account number. The situation is further safeguarded as banks will only respond to enquiries from other banks, so you must address your reference through your own bank.

REQUEST FOR A BANKERS REFERENCE

<your bank>
<Street> <Town & postcode>
September 18.20XX

Dear Sir,

Re: D W COMPUTER SUPPLIES of <Street> <Town> <County>

We have been approached by the above named for a trade credit account and would be obliged if you would request his bankers for their opinion, in confidence, and without responsibility, as to the suitability of the above mentioned firm in the sum of (amount of proposed credit limit). For the period of (state your trade terms).

Their bankers, and account details are: (Name, address, sorting code, and account number)

Thank you for your assistance,

Yours faithfully,
PROPRIETOR.

Interpretation of replies

It is essential that you get the bank's opinion on a specific sum and the proposed period of credit - a general opinion is of little use to you. The following wordings are commonly used by banks and should be interpreted as indicated. Many reports will begin with the following wording:

> ⚠️ **CAUTION** Companies can submit their accounts to 'Companies House' past recognised cut-off dates. Take care that the information provided by a credit reference agency is not outdated.

- respectable
- trustworthy
- properly construed company.......etc.

BANK REFERENCE REPLIES

Wording	Interpretation
• Undoubted	Credit worthy for substantial sums
• Good	Figure requested is normal for customer
• Should prove good	Figure requested is a little higher than the bank would like to see
• Trustworthy, suitable, safe etc • Should prove trustworthy • While we do not think they would enter a commitment they could not see their way to fulfil.	Where these and other adjectives are given as a central opinion, a cautionary stance is suggested. All these statements indicate the bank is unwilling to commit itself. While there may be good reason for this, treat with extreme caution any new customer with no track record.
• Unable to speak for your figures • Fully committed/employed	Further enquiries are recommended Customer has tight cash flow or no funds, in other words, not credit-worthy

With regard to the third item on the previous page, it must be assumed any company that has been properly established could justify this phrase. Rather, it is the secondary statement that will be of importance in these circumstances.

On the other hand, if the bank does not specifically answer for the amount enquired about, or refers to the directors as opposed to the company, and then these reports should also be considered as cautionary.

Interpreting business accounts

> **TIP** Your local trade association or chamber of commerce can be good, although informal, sources of credit information.

It is easy enough to request a copy of a potential customer's account, but it will prove a pointless exercise if you do not understand how to interpret it.

Fortunately, you do not need to be an accountant to master the mysteries of a firm's accounts. The profit and loss account, and especially the balance sheet, can be an invaluable window into the financial status of your new customer, alongside your other investigations.

However, a single set of accounts is of little value on it's own. At least three years' figures are required to judge if the business is expanding or not. It must be remembered that a firm's accounts only reflect the status of the company at a given date.

The salient factors when reading and understanding a customer's accounts are the equations referred to as ratios. Each ratio should always be compared against previous years' results to discover if the business is improving or declining. There are a number of equations that can be used, but the ones of particular interest when considering an application for trade credit are as follows:

◆ Profit/Sales ratio

This ratio indicates the cost-effectiveness of running the whole business. It will illustrate the management's attempts to keep costs under control, particularly if sales have shown a decrease against earlier years. Ideally, the percentage of profit measured against sales should be increasing. A static figure

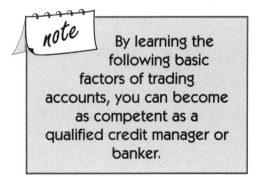

By learning the following basic factors of trading accounts, you can become as competent as a qualified credit manager or banker.

shows the firm is holding it's own, but you should be on the lookout for any sign of deterioration. Any evidence of such signs will require close supervision, if you decide to grant credit in these instances.

◆ Sales/Net assets

This ratio measures the ability of the management to generate profitable sales. A higher ratio over previous years is to be looked upon favourably, providing the increase is steady. A rapid escalation from one year to another should be a warning that the business is over-trading. Any firm caught up in over-trading may have difficulty in paying bills if a sudden drop in sales is experienced.

◆ Trade debtors/Sales

This ratio will tell you how much control your prospective customer has over his or her own trade debtors. This equation should be weighed against what can be considered normal credit terms for the type of industry the customer is engaged in. In some business sectors, 60 days credit is not unusual. But if their customers are taking 60 days or longer to pay in a sector where 30 days is the norm, caution must be your key word when establishing credit limits. If you find these customers of your potential customer are taking more time to pay than you approved, it will be a sign of future trouble. Firms who are lax in collecting their own receivables tend to resolve the situation by taking longer to pay themselves.

◆ **Assets/Liabilities**

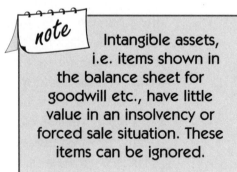

note Intangible assets, i.e. items shown in the balance sheet for goodwill etc., have little value in an insolvency or forced sale situation. These items can be ignored.

When giving consideration to the value of assets, you must bear in mind that not all assets are liquid. So in assessing the availability of working capital, a ratio of say 3/1 or more, that is to say the business has three times more assets than liabilities, can be considered excellent. 1.5/1 or 2/1 is advantageous, 1.25/1 needs a cautious approach, and anything below this level would require close investigation. Some equations can initially seem acceptable, but when further checks are made, the results can be found deceptive. This could be due to:

If you are still undecided about a potential customer, despite various reports and analysis exercises, visit their premises. Its condition should indicate whether they are expanding or contracting.

- excessive stocks of raw materials
- large holdings of slow moving stock
- the extent of unfinished work in progress
- unpaid taxes

These are all indications your new customer is a poor business risk. Having said that, it is possible to conduct a very profitable relationship with a firm of this nature, provided you are prepared to closely monitor this type of customer.

Final analysis

Assessing a customer's financial status should not only be carried out when they first get taken on board. Situations change rapidly in business, so regular reviews ought to be undertaken. This will not only ensure you are taking advantage of all possible sales growth, but should also prove that you are not exposing your business to undue risk.

Whilst it is desirable for these checks to be undertaken on a regular basis, it is understood they are time consuming. Investing in an appropriate software package with access to external agencies could well be an advisable alternative. Preventing bad debt from arising is sound business practice. Assessing the credit rating of every customer will help you achieve this goal.

Reconciling accounts

When undertaken on a regular basis, this important audit function will ensure the amount your customer states they owe you agrees with what you believe to be due. A reconciled account must confirm:

note Customers do not usually raise queries until payment is due. It is up to you to bring them to light prior to this time.

- all receipts have been properly allocated
- only authorised credit notes have been raised
- customer complaints have been resolved
- invoices have been sent to the customer

CAUTION It's important to have a fully reconciled account nearby when new orders arrive from a customer close to their credit limit.

Reconciling customer accounts should become a regular habit. Monthly auditing will be necessary for customers with a heavy volume of debit and credit transactions. For your smaller customers, the frequency of audit will depend on how often invoices are raised. The annual audit by the firm's auditors will confirm the sales ledger is being maintained properly. However, you need to undertake your own account reconciliation and not rely on annual audits.

Aged analysis

Every month, an aged sales ledger analysis must be completed. Computerised systems will automatically perform this function. An aged sales ledger report will highlight the oldest outstanding items in the sales ledger that require immediate attention. This analysis functions as a useful collection tool, particularly when used in conjunction with the customer's history and diary report. It can also highlight any potential problems between you and your customer.

Aged sales ledger				Month ended:	31 August XXXX	
Name	Acc No	current	30 days	60 days	90 days+	Total due
DW Comp Sups	00032	422.24	279.88	107.08	55.18	864.38
PA Toys	00124	195.14	374.77		78.91	648.83
A N Other Stores	00125	714.68	211.58			926.26
Sales Accounting	00189	208.56	84.14	475.63		768.33
Rogue Cars	00194			20.30	632.64	652.94

Invoices, statements, credit & debit notes

Credit and debit notes should be treated as cash, so they'll be dealt with first. These two documents are raised as a consequence of a customer's dispute arising from either:

- returned stock (delivered by mistake)
- short delivery
- damaged goods
- incorrect pricing

CAUTION Don't let customers or staff abuse the use of credit or debit notes. These notes can only be issued after a complaint has been checked and an error confirmed.

These notes can only be issued after a complaint has been checked and an error confirmed.

There are a many other reasons you could list for issuing a debit or credit note. It is not necessary to wait until your customer complains to issue a credit note. If you discover an error in an invoice or delivery, making an amendment by way of a credit note before your customer becomes aware of the problem can only improve customer relations and speed up payment.

Debit notes

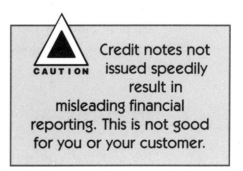

Although the use of debit notes is on the increase, this practice should be discouraged whenever possible. A debit note is the customers' way of taking credit against their own account query. Such notes are useful

Credit notes not issued speedily result in misleading financial reporting. This is not good for you or your customer.

in a sense, since they provoke you into swift action. It must be tactfully pointed out to your customer, however, that debit note deductions from their account will not be permitted without your prior consent. This consent may only be given once you or a member of your staff has approved the debit/credit item.

Credit notes

Credit notes may only be agreed upon to rectify an invoicing, delivery error or omission. The use of credit notes allows your customer to offset certain sums against what they owe, as shown in the credit note against the balance of a specified invoice. Speedy resolution of customers' disputes and the issue of authorised credit notes are vital to ensure prompt payment of the remainder of the amount due. All credit notes should be given a number quite distinct from invoice numbers. A credit note's make up is the same as an invoice, except for two things: it is usually printed in a different colour to avoid confusion, and the words 'credit note' replace 'invoice'.

Invoices and Statements

Timing is important when producing invoices and statements. For further information, see the pages relating to cut-off dates and reconciliation. On every invoice, statement, or credit note you send to your customer, your terms of trade should be clearly stated. These clearly printed terms act as a constant remainder to your customers of the importance you place on receiving prompt payment every month.

Each document plays a vital role in recording and controlling your debtors. Whilst these documents compliment each other, we'll study them one at a time.

Invoices

For collection purposes, an invoice handed to a customer at the time of delivery is ideal. Unfortunately, this only works if there are no errors in the document. To avoid mistakes and reduce the opportunity for your customer to complain, invoices must be sent as soon as possible after delivery.

Drivers, or transport contractors must not be left in any doubt about the importance of returning delivery documentation promptly.

An invoice must explicitly list the goods delivered, the amount due (including VAT), and must confirm your terms of trade. Whenever possible it must also clearly display:

- the customer's order number
- the despatch note number
- the invoice number
- where payment is to be made
- the currency (for export orders)

It will assist you both if a remittance advice is included with every invoice and statement. Always send important documents via first class post.

D W COMPUTER SUPPLIES

<street> <town> <post code> <telephone>

INVOICE

Invoice to: Deliver to:

Order No: Despatch note No:
Currency: Invoice No:

Date:	Description	Quantity	Unit price	Total
			sub total:	
			VAT:	
			Amount due:	

Terms of payment 30 days from date of invoice.

D W COMPUTER SUPPLIES
<street> <town> <post code> <telephone>

STATEMENT OF ACCOUNT

<customer's name>   Account No:
<street>   Credit limit:
<town> <post code>

Date:	Description	Amount	Balance
24.8.XX	Invoice No 0868*	£210. 40	£210. 40*
3.9.XX	Invoice No 0988	122. 83	333. 23
4.9.XX	Invoice No 0989	336. 33	669. 56
16.9.XX	Credit note No 052	14. 81	654. 75
30.9.XX	Cash Advice note No 37	122. 83	531. 92

Items * are overdue and must be paid by return of post.
Terms of payment 30 days from date of invoice.

Statements

Statements provide an excellent reminder to your customers of the amount outstanding and when you expect payment. They are also ideal for reconciling your accounts with your customers'. They should clearly show:

- a record of all unpaid invoices
- all cash receipts since last statement date
- disputed invoices
- terms of trade
- overdue items
- credit notes issued

> **TIP** Check all statements for accuracy before sending to customers. This procedure allows all zero balances to be removed, thus saving on postage. Send the smaller account statements by second class post to reduce costs, if these are numerable.

Ensuring all items are posted to their respective ledgers daily and keeping to a strict time-table for cut-off dates each month allows you time to reconcile your accounts accurately. Accurate accounts early in the month are most likely to become paid accounts by the end of the month.

Measuring what is owed to you

Unless you know how much debt is outstanding at various moments in time, you will never know if your customers are paying you regularly. Discovering how much money is outstanding can be measured in two ways, the 'Exhaust Method', which measures the days sales outstanding (DSO), or the 'Percentage Debt Summary'. The second option is a more reliable gauge of debtors than the first, which can be distorted by the volume of invoices issued in the previous month.

DEFINITION

The Exhaust Method uses a formula that relates to a ratio of the sales ledger balance against the total value of recent sales. With a ratio of days sales outstanding (DSO) of say 65 days, all your customers are, on average, taking this length of time to pay you after receiving your goods. Offering trade credit terms of 30 days in this situation is not good - you should be aiming to reduce this figure.

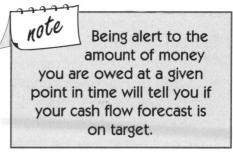

note Being alert to the amount of money you are owed at a given point in time will tell you if your cash flow forecast is on target.

To calculate the DSO, let us assume at the end of August your total sales ledger debts amounted to £1,000,000. The example below shows how the DSO of 65 days was arrived at.

EXHAUST METHOD - DAYS SALES OUTSTANDING	
Total debt at Apr 30	£1,000,000
less APRIL sales (30 days)	460,000
equals	540,000
less MARCH sales unpaid (31 days)	480,000
equals	60,000

The balance of £60,000 represents February sales which remain unpaid namely (4) days. Adding the number of day's sales unpaid over a three-month period gives you a DSO of:

$$(30) + (31) + (4) = 65$$

Although widely used as a measure of outstanding debt at stated points in time, this method is unreliable because the older a debt gets, the harder it becomes to collect. It can also hide such things as:

- old debts
- long unsettled disputes
- difficult and bad debts

Percentage debt report

DEFINITION

This ratio measures the aged debt balance remaining on the sales ledger at the end of each month against the actual sales totals for the same period. This result is unaffected by any outside influences, and can be relied upon as it shows the actual percent of sales unpaid each month. To display this ratio you need to place the monthly sales figures in chronological order. Now range the aged balances diagonally so the remaining debt each month is in line with its corresponding sales total. Once arranged in this fashion, it is a simple matter to calculate the percentage of sales remaining unpaid. A demonstration of this calculation is as follows:

PERCENTAGE DEBT REPORT - £'000's								
	SALES		MONTH 1		MONTH 2		MONTH 3	
Month	£	%	£	%	£	%	£	%
July	420	100	273	65	60	14	6.5	1.5
August	480	100	413	86	240	50		
September	460	100	322	70				

Divide 60,000 by 420,000 and multiply the answer by 100. This calculation gives you the percentage of February sales that remain unpaid.

Using this system, it is much easier to detect whether or not the current debt is being collected. Additionally, you should be able to concentrate your collection effects to any poor performing area within the sales ledger utilising this system of measurement.

Collecting by telephone

4

Chapter 4

Collecting by telephone

What you'll find in this chapter:

⏵ Preparing for the call

⏵ Developing two way dialogues

⏵ Getting a commitment

⏵ Dealing with customers' excuses

⏵ Preventing late payment

⏵ Getting money out of reluctant payers

It is all very well selling the best goods or services, but if you do not get paid, why bother? To make sure you are paid on time, you must:

- use pragmatic collection methods
- take measures to prevent late payment
- learn how to deal with difficult customers

The telephone is by far the best collection tool you have. Its cost effectiveness lies in its immediacy and proficiency for stimulating the correct

---

response with the first call, thus offering a spontaneous and persistent method of cash collection.

> **TIP** Letters can be lost, put out of sight, even ignored, but it is difficult to ignore a telephone request for payment. Plan every call carefully and support your dialogue by having all relevant paperwork to hand.

There is, however, a downside to telephone collecting, especially for the unwary and the timid. It is easy for a customer to make excuses, and in some cases, be downright rude. To some people, the telephone is impersonal, but in the right hands it can be a virtual money machine, as you'll see as this chapter unfolds.

Preparing for the call

If your sales ledger is not computerised, have in front of you, in hard copy form, the customer's account details before picking up the telephone. If using a computerised system, you will have displayed on the screen:

- a current statement
- the customers history report
- aged sales ledger analysis

By having this information to hand, you'll avoid frustrating your customer unnecessarily. There is nothing more annoying for a customer than to be repeatedly put 'on hold' when having a conversation, simply because you haven't got all the fact to hand during a telephone call.

Your attitude must be right

How you come across to your customer over the telephone is important. This means you must be assertive, open, honest, direct, and show understanding of your customers' problems. Stand up for your rights, without violating the rights of your customer. Your posture is also important, so be relaxed, sit upright and smile. Ask positive questions, be fluent and emphasise key words. Above all do not:

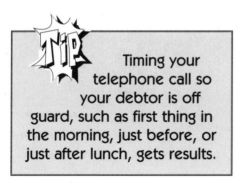

Timing your telephone call so your debtor is off guard, such as first thing in the morning, just before, or just after lunch, gets results.

- show contempt
- be patronising
- become aggressive
- be submissive
- believe your opinions are more important than theirs

Your voice needs to be steady, warm, and most of all, sincere. Always address your contact by their Christian name and be friendly. People like doing things for friends, including making sure you are paid on time.

Now! let's make that call.

Developing two way dialogues

To be effective when collecting via the telephone, you need to maintain constant control of the conversation. Always be polite, never be abusive or make threats you do not intend to follow through. Above all else SMILE, it really does get through to your customer, creating a relaxed ambience.

Take a little time prior to dialling your customer's telephone number. Use this period to run through in your mind what you want to say and exactly what you expect the call to achieve. Being aware of how your customer operates will give you confidence. Pick up the receiver, take one or two deep breaths, dial your customer's number and ask for your contact by name. Speak slowly, clearly and with a hint of determination.

To get a two-way dialogue flowing, commence the conversation by mentioning the amount of debt. Then continue by asking open ended questions, such as:

- Do you agree with this figure?
- When did you say you sent the cheque?
- What was the amount you sent?
- Who did you say was sorting out your query?

CAUTION Be tactful. However the debtor behaves, you must acknowledge all comments and always speak politely.

Getting a commitment

Do not ask the type of questions that require a yes or no reply, until the time when you want to get a commitment from your customer. For example:

- You did receive our invoice in September, Miss Z?
- Do you agree the outstanding balance of £375?
- You will be sending a cheque for that amount to reach us by the 28th of this month?

Had your customer answered 'NO' to any of the above questions, you would respond by enquiring into the reason. If the customer replies "it's because we're waiting for a credit note", as soon as the call is over, remedy the problem in the shortest time-scale possible and recall the debtor.

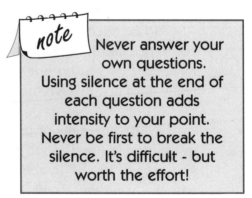

note Never answer your own questions. Using silence at the end of each question adds intensity to your point. Never be first to break the silence. It's difficult - but worth the effort!

Be ready at all times to respond to any excuses in a positive manner. Keep a note of what was promised on your customer's history and diary record. Include the dates any follow up action will be required. This will most certainly include the date the customer said you would receive his cheque. If it doesn't arrive on the day stated, call him back straight away. What you should expect to get from the call is:

- confirmation of the amount owed
- confirmation that the customer has no complaints
- acknowledgement that all of your invoices will be passed for payment before the customer's cut-off date
- their agreement to send a cheque
- the date the cheque will be posted

Once the customer confirms they will be sending a cheque, insist that it be sent via first class post. One further point: make certain the customer repeats the promises they have just made to you, such as how much the cheque will be worth and when it will be mailed. Under no circumstances say it for them.

 During or immediately after the call, while the details are still fresh in your mind, jot the salient points of the conversation onto the customer diary report. Include the date, the type of contact such as telephone, letter or fax, who you spoke to, and what was agreed or promised, including any promises you made. Complete your entry by entering the date of any follow up action. For example:

- the date the cheque is due
- the date by which you arranged to call back with an answer to their query

After using the customer contact form for just a few months, you should see a pattern emerge. At a glance you'll be able to spot those telling lies and be able to distinguish between the customers making feeble excuses and the ones who are experiencing real difficulties.

Always call your customer back on the date you stated. If a debtor is experiencing difficulties meeting their obligations, it's better to accept a smaller amount for the time being than nothing at all.

It's good to listen

One of the most important, yet overlooked aspects of telephone collecting, is not talking, but listening. You have ears, so use them actively! Evaluate what your customer is saying - discover what he actually means. Anticipate what the customer is trying to say and review mentally what has already been said. Speculate on the real message and try to understand any difficulties your customer is experiencing.

Skilled telephone collectors are always polite without demeaning themselves. They act instead of react to situations by:

- telling the customer what is expected of them
- being precise
- being concise
- projecting credibility at all times

> **TIP**
> During the call, maintain consistency in controlling the conversation. Remain calm and sympathetic, but be firm and stay positive. Never argue with a customer- you can't win. Appreciate their problems in a way that is neutral and ask what you can do to help.

Having a clear objective at the start of the call will get a firm commitment from your customer to pay what is owed to you. This should become second nature to you. Asking open-ended questions will gain your customers' willingness to co-operate. Once you have achieved this, re-confirm with the debtor the amount being paid and the date the cheque will be in the mail.

Dealing with customers' excuses

Whatever service you give your customers, there will always be a few who will try to 'Buck the System', doing everything in their power to delay paying you for as long as possible. Unfortunately, if you let this type of customer get away with paying late once, chances are they will take every opportunity that arises in the future to use your firm as a source of interest free credit. When faced with these customers you must:

- be persistent
- not be afraid to hurt their feelings
- be prepared to counter-act their excuses
- keep referring to the sum required
- be compelling, let them see you expect payment today

Should they try to avert your attention, be professional, and return to the matter in hand - payment in full.

Overcoming excuses

Comedians rehearse 'Ad libs' until their quips become second nature. Likewise, you need to develop a repartee that permits anyone phoning on behalf of your company to have a positive approach to reasons given for non-payment, and not accept them at face value.

note

Be objective when first confronted with an excuse. Ask yourself if the reason given is genuine or just a delaying ploy.

The aim of contacting your customers is to get them to commit themselves to a cheque. Your customers have received the goods ordered and have had use of them, so why must you wait for the money due to you? Never adopt a defensive attitude or show any sign of weakness. Instead, be positive, friendly, and treat each person on the other end of the telephone as an individual. Always keep a note of any new excuses you come across. Rehearse your retort, practice how you will respond when faced with the same rationale again.

TOP TEN EXCUSES AND SUGGESTED RESPONSES

Customer excuse	*Suggested reply*
Waiting for cheque to be signed Or, the person who signs the cheque is away.	Who normally signs your cheques? Perhaps I should speak to your manager or Finance Director. Does that mean you can't get paid this month?
Lost the invoice please send a copy.	Of course! I'll fax it to you right away, and call back this afternoon.
We have cash flow problems	I can appreciate your position. But our terms of trade are -(state terms). We do expect £xxx now. If I contact your MD, maybe we can agree a payment schedule.
The cheque is in the post	Thank you! Can I just confirm the details so I can check it hasn't gone astray? Or, could you cancel that cheque and issue another today, first class post?
You stated an incorrect price	I see from my records that you mentioned this two weeks ago. I sent a credit note and a replacement invoice ten days ago addressed to you. Now let's see, the balance due is £xxx?

Customer excuse	*Suggested reply*
Our computer system has broken down	I can sympathise with your problem. When our system went down, we had to revert to issuing manual cheques again. Now I believe the balance outstanding is?
We're waiting for a new chequebook	Don't worry about that. I'll just give you our bank details, and you can arrange for an electronic transfer. I have a balance of £xxx? Do you agree?
The invoice is in dispute	We have no record of any dispute in our log. Give me the details and I'll sort it out today and come back to you tomorrow.
We only pay on 60/90 day terms not 30	We know some firms have different terms, but our credit terms were pointed out and confirmed with your buyer when we took your order. Please transfer me to your MD.
You missed the cheque run	Nothing to do, but learn how your customers operates and keep proper records. See Chapter One and the following pages.

Only by asking probing questions will you test the strength of an excuse. Now repeat your request for payment. If your customer continues to pursue their reason for not paying, tell them you will investigate their problem and call back.

Always call back on the day promised, even if it is to simply tell your customer you need a little more time to get the problem sorted out. These little gestures let your customers know you value their patronage. If they go off-track, giving differing reasons for not paying, then you'll know they are only making excuses, so you must be a little more forceful in pressing for payment.

Other questions you may ask which will help you get to the truth are feeling questions. Probing and feeling questions can be listed as:

- who and why?
- how much?
- when or where?
- is it important?
- what do you mean?
- what is the reason?
- what do you think?

Background knowledge

Knowing how your customers work can assist you when confronted with an obvious pretext. Say you are speaking to the bought ledger controller who states they are waiting for invoices to be approved. You can ask to be transferred to the person who approves your invoices by name. A brief conversation with that person may speed up the process. Information such as this is invaluable to you. It will usually be found on your customer's history report, so any change in a customer's staff requires this form to be updated. Understanding your customers is important.

CAUTION Telephone collection does not have to be aggressive. Using threats usually brings about a negative attitude from your debtors.

Repeat your terms of trade when facing evasion of payment. If you are still unsure about the reasons given, ask for part payment while you check into their query, and tell them when you'll call them back. If you had not fully prepared your call by checking the disputes log, do so now. Supposing you see their complaint listed, you can call you customer back right away and explain what is happening to the dispute. If it isn't listed, complete a dispute form and set the dispute system in motion.

Preventing late payment

In the British Isles, the average time span from the point of sale until receipt of payment is 77 days. Considering trade credit terms are usually 30 days, this is indeed a poor record. Whilst some firms pay quicker than average, some companies are paying later than the 77 days quoted. Since we've discovered that permitting your customer to dictate payment terms leads to business failure more often than anything else, what can you do to reverse this trend? You should:

- take the initiative with collections
- start your collection practices early
- remove the excuses customers use to delay payment

You have seen what late payment can cost your business. Preventing accounts becoming overdue is far easier, and offers better business prospects, than chasing for late payments.

note Collecting should be a customer service. By starting the procedures early you shouldn't even have to ask for the money.

Your first duty is to your business and employees. Taking fundamental precautions makes sense, but you will not have eliminated all the risks. The next step is to ensure you get paid per your terms. There is nothing shameful in expecting to get paid for the goods or services delivered. You will pay your workers at the end of every week or month for their labour, without them having to demand it, so why should you wait for your money? There are some businesses that deliberately

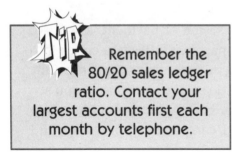

Remember the 80/20 sales ledger ratio. Contact your largest accounts first each month by telephone.

retain payment until they are asked for it. Therefore, the earlier you start the collection process each month, the faster you will be paid.

Remove those excuses

Starting your collection procedure two or three weeks before payment is due will not upset your customers, providing you do it tactfully. In the course of your first telephone call, say a few days after they have received their invoices from you, you must:

- confirm the goods have been delivered
- establish there were no shortages or breakages
- agree the invoice totals are correct
- confirm the invoice will be processed before the customer's cut off date

You will note, the aim of the conversation early in the collection cycle was not demanding, nor asking for payment. Instead, this call establishes your customer had no complaints, that they got what they ordered, when they wanted it, and there were no mistakes with the invoice.

If they had stated, for example, that the invoice totals were incorrect, or only three dozen items were delivered instead of the four dozen they were invoiced, you would have sufficient time using your disputes system to rectify the problem before the period of credit expired. This leaves your customer no option but to pay on time. They cannot say the invoice was wrong, can they? Because you have checked it with them.

You have taken away the excuses customer rely upon to delay payment.

CAUTION Your collection policy must be flexible. Don't insist only certain value debtors are contacted by telephone each month, especially if there is a drop in sales.

Telephone techniques to use

After you have selected your largest customers, they should be graded by the amount they owe, not the age of the debt. Giving priority to your collections in this manner will prevent debts becoming old in the future. Once you have graded the smaller customers in a similar manner, you may decide to telephone some of the larger of the smaller accounts, if time permits. All customers with a balance above £2,500 could be classified for collection one month. The next month, because the number of active customers has reduced, you may want to telephone all those accounts with balances in excess of £1,000.

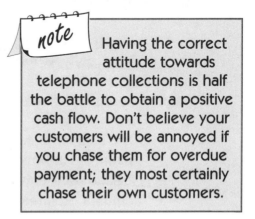

note Having the correct attitude towards telephone collections is half the battle to obtain a positive cash flow. Don't believe your customers will be annoyed if you chase them for overdue payment; they most certainly chase their own customers.

Having a firm collection policy that includes:

* set collection targets
* a time table for calls
* using Christian names wherever possible
* follow up calls
* using non-productive times of the day for allocating cash ensures you will have a positive incoming cash flow each month. For maximum effect, set times for your telephone calls and times for allocating the cash receipts. Telephone collecting costs money, so it is important to restrict it to those times that will give you the utmost advantage.

Monitoring collection activity

It will be meaningful to monitor the telephone collection activity. It does not matter if it's only you, a part-time book-keeper or a team of credit controllers. This will ensure the right number of customers is being contacted on a daily basis. In fact, this is especially true if you are employing someone to look after your sales ledger, since payments received from a few large debtors can mask inactivity by your staff.

> **note** It is not only large businesses that need to be alerted to collection performance. Small firms must be reassured constantly that their cash flow will not take a sudden dive when least expected.

The only thing required to monitor this activity is for a simple 'Achievement Summary' to be completed each day which will confirm:

- the number of calls made
- name of customer called
- balance of account
- amount promised, and date sent
- date payment received

The accuracy of the summaries can be checked against the comments on the customer's history and contact record.

Getting money out of reluctant payers

There will always be an odd handful of customers who will use every excuse in the book to delay paying until the last possible moment - and then some.

Irrespective of the level of service you offer, or quality of your goods, there is always someone who thinks he can outsmart you. If a customer continually and deliberately puts off paying you, then your gloves should come off. Now you are embroiled in a battle of wits! In these circumstances, there is no reason at all why you should not use the same tactics as your debtor. Here are a few 'little white lies' you could use.

➤ 'As a favour to me.' If you've established a friendly relationship with the bought ledger operator, pretending you have an irate manager breathing down your neck may prompt the release of your cheque sooner rather than later. This wee ploy can work wonders.

➤ 'It's bonus time.' Tell the offending customer that only money arriving before a certain date (say 7 to 10 days time) will be counted towards your bonus. If they'll send their cheque straight away, you'll be able to take your frail old mother away. Making them feel guilty can also work.

➤ 'I'm afraid our auditors have picked your account at random.' Anybody who has worked in an accounts office knows the pressures auditors put on staff. Tell your customer that they are even now checking that your credit control procedures are working. If the customer puts a cheque into the post right away, you'll be able to leave them in peace.

➤ 'We think our computer sent out some incorrect statements. Yours may be one of them - would you please check.' Hopefully the customer will then verify there is nothing wrong with their statement, they'll confirm that they agree the amount owed to you, and that there are no problems outstanding. Now, ask for the cheque.

Bear this in mind: persistence, firmness, politeness and the occasional white lie will always win in the end.

A WORD OF WARNING

Only use the above suggestions on the hard core debtor, the one always paying late and making excuses. For the rest, only the truth will do.

Collecting by post and fax

5

Chapter 5

Collecting by post and fax

What you'll find in this chapter:

➠ Dealing with small debts

➠ Letter cycles that work

➠ What your letters are up against

➠ Points to avoid

➠ Final Demand

Thanks to computers and the word processor, collecting by post has almost become an art. Gone are the days when printed stereotype reminders were sent out at regular intervals. The time gap between these types of letter was such you could set your calendar by them. Now collection letters can be produced and addressed to a specific person in seconds, with each one looking as if it been personally written to the recipient.

Generally speaking, all small businesses can now afford to invest in some form of computerised accounting and word processing systems. For matter-of-course accounting practices they are invaluable, but when it comes to organising a collection letter cycle they really prove how extremely useful an investment they are.

The cost of any of these systems should not be a factor these days. A suitable computer (PC's) with a printer can be bought from £500 to £600. More powerful models will cost less than a thousand. If you are still worried about this cost to your new business, try the second-hand market. Reliable

models with years of useful life left in them can be picked up at auction or through computer magazines for a couple of hundred pounds. So you see, there really is no excuse for not having a professional collection system in operation.

In a majority of businesses it will not be possible to contact every customer each month by telephone. Therefore, whilst letters cannot be as personal as the telephone, they can be just as effective if used correctly. Such letters should always be addressed to an individual; this is where your customer history and contact record is useful. Failing that, use a job title.

Letters, like your telephone calls, must be firm but polite. Collection letters should be kept simple and direct, never any longer than one page in length. When writing, always think about long term relationships, so word your letter carefully. All the rules relating to telephone debt collection apply equally to collecting by post.

On the other hand, a fax message tends to be accepted as more urgent than a letter. Faxes are therefore very effectual against slow or lazy purchase ledger staff, particularly if sent to senior managers, containing a threat to cut off supplies.

Dealing with small debts

Obviously, the small customer who goes out of business will not have the same impact on your liquidity as a larger customer who "goes bust". Nevertheless, small businesses can be vital to your success, so small accounts cannot be overlooked. Certainly they must not be permitted to become overdue. A number a small debtors each owing perhaps between £75 to £150 can add up to a substantial sum if left to accumulate.

Most firms have a cycle of letters to send to overdue accounts. Many tend to share the same predictable features, saying the same thing, sending each and every letter 7 or ten days apart. Amazingly, they never seem to start this cycle until an account is overdue! With this situation in mind, it is a good idea to change the content, change the style, and alternate the frequency that your letters are sent. Amendments should be made three or four times a year. Not allowing an archetype to emerge will keep your customers guessing. They should not be able to spot any trend and thereby profit from it.

Letter cycles that work

It is of little use to send a continuous stream of letters chasing late payment with no forethought. To be effective, a letter cycle should contain no more than three letters. Additionally, the cycles must be flexible; otherwise the routine becomes too predictable for customers. The crafty ones will soon learn to ignore the first couple of reminder letters they receive. If payment is not forthcoming within a three-letter cycle, it is unlikely that five or six letters will produce the desired result, so more stringent methods will be required.

The timing of your letters is important to maximise cash receipts, just as it is with telephone collections. Your first letter should accompany a customer's statement. For the best results, it should be written with the following criteria in mind. Is the letter:

- personalised, i.e. addressed to the person handling your account with a written signature?

- a request, not a demand for payment?

- informing the customer what must be paid, when, and where?

- giving the latest date for raising disputes?

- providing your customer with a contact name and telephone number?

The first letter

All collections letters should be brief, to the point, and polite. Do not make any threats or demands unless you intend to carry them out. Be specific. Avoid jargon such as 'other action will be taken'. If you are going to sue your customer or pass the account to a debt collector, say so.

When you use the telephone to make your collections, you can instantly be informed of each customer's situation. If you use letters for collection, you will not immediately be made aware of any difficulties facing the customer. Unsurprisingly, your customer's difficulties are going to be more important to them than your letter. Some of the difficulties they're facing could be:

- their own customers are paying late

- the breakdown of vital machinery or computers

- staff are off sick

- the tax inspector is chasing them

Therefore, design your first letter to simply establish that there are no problems with the goods or services you supplied. This is also the time to confirm that they agree with the figure you say is owing. An example of a suitable first letter to accompany the monthly statement can be found on the next page.

INITIAL COLLECTION LETTER

D W Computer Supplies
Anywhere Street,
Any Town 12ZZ 34YY.   September 30.20XX

Dear

Re: Account No: WX 0098721
BALANCE: £1,758. 34

    I have pleasure in enclosing your current monthly statement. Please reconcile this with the invoice(s) in your possession and inform me of any discrepancies no later than the 8th October 20XX.
    If I do not hear from you by the above date, it will be assumed you will be paying the balance as stated, in full, before the expiry of the credit period.
    Respectfully, I would draw your attention to our terms of trade, which are stated on the enclosed statement.
    Please enclose the remittance slip below with your cheque and/or dispute.
    Thank you for you co-operation.

Yours sincerely,

PROPRIETOR or CREDIT CONTROLLER

- -

Account No: WX0098721   Balance £: 1,758. 34
Cheque enclosed valued at: £..............................
Part/full payment is being withheld because:

....

....

Signed: Position:
Date: Telephone No: Ext:
Please list the invoice numbers your payment represents on the back of this slip.

All correspondence in your letter cycle, with the exception of the first one, should re-confirm your terms of trade. These terms will be clearly stated on the attached statement of account.

Follow up letter

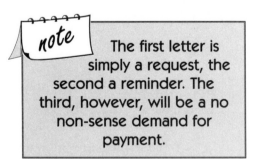

This letter must confirm the amount of overdue debt that you require to be paid by return of post, together with the amount due to be paid at the end of that month.

The first letter is simply a request, the second a reminder. The third, however, will be a no non-sense demand for payment.

Again, this letter should be personally addressed to the same person as your last letter. It wouldn't hurt to also address a copy to your contact's departmental manager or employer and send it separately. The following is an example of a typical second letter:

SECOND COLLECTION LETTER

D W Computer Supplies
Anywhere Street
Any Town 12ZZ 34YY   October 11.20XX

Dear

Re: Account No: WX0098721
Balance: £1,758. 34

I refer to my letter dated the 30th September 20XX. Not receiving any response to this letter, I assume you have no outstanding queries regarding the account. Payment in full is expected as follows.

The overdue amount of £422.12 must be paid by return of post. The balance, which amounts to £1,336.22, must be paid on or before the 29th of October 20XX.

If you now wish to dispute an outstanding invoice, I can confirm that this dispute will be investigated fully, and if the dispute is substantiated any overpayment will be refunded without delay. In the meantime, we expect this invoice to be paid in full.

Yours sincerely,

Proprietor/Credit controller.

Incorporate payment/complaint slip as per first collection letter.

Ensuring that disputed invoices are raised within a predetermined time scale in a letter cycle gives you sufficient time to resolve any dispute before payment becomes due. Unlike a telephone call, when you become aware of a problem immediately, monitoring the response your collection letters generate takes time. It will take you longer to learn the details of a customer's complaint, so you must plan accordingly.

Final letters

Your final letter most definitely must be the last letter of your cycle. Do not, as some firms do, send a final letter that is then followed by a final demand etc. If the debt remains unpaid, you ought to do exactly as you have previously stated you will do.

> **CAUTION** Never bluff. Threatening to do something and not following through with it may work once, but debtors will get to know future threats can be ignored.

The interval between the second and final letter must be varied from month to month. One month the letters might be ten days apart, the next seven, another month only four or five days, and so forth. A sample final letter is displayed on page 86.

note Only one exception to the final demand rule should ever be permitted: you have used an outside collection agency that proved to be unsuccessful. Either you or this agency acting on your instructions should send a further demand confirming your intention to sue. Your solicitor would also give your customer a final opportunity to pay before actually instigating any proceedings.

Telephone first

It is desirable to precede the final letter with a telephone call. However, if this fails to procure the result you wanted, you're left with no other option but to send the final letter. A large number of your customers will have responded to your earlier letters, therefore the number of telephone calls you will be required to make will be minimal.

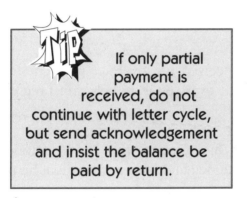

If only partial payment is received, do not continue with letter cycle, but send acknowledgement and insist the balance be paid by return.

If you still need to send the final letter, it should be addressed to the manager of your customer's bought ledger department with a copy faxed to the financial director.

FINAL DEMAND LETTER

D W Computer Supplies
Anywhere Street,
Any Town 12ZZ 34YY   October 20.20XX

Dear Sirs,

Re: Account No: WX0098721
   Overdue balance: £422.12

I am surprised not to have received the overdue payment from you, which is re-stated above. Having made every effort to help you, I regret to note the account still remains unpaid.

Unless payment is received at this office by the 27th of October 20XX, further supplies to you will be suspended and your account will be passed to our outside collection agency.

or

Unless payment is received by the 27th of October 20XX, our solicitors will be instructed to commence legal proceedings against you. No further warning will be given.

Your immediate payment of £422.12 will avoid this distasteful action and prevent any extra expenses incurred in this process from being added to your account.

Yours faithfully

PROPRIETOR/CREDIT MANAGER

Faxing your debtors' finance or managing director this letter will most probably make it unlikely you will need to resort to the threats embodied in the letter. Remember what was said earlier: never use any threat as a bluff. Always be prepared to follow through with what you stated you would do if they failed to pay as you instructed. Late payment costs you dearly. You are entitled to expect payment when you want it and be unhappy with a customer's failure to pay on time. Do not expect a reply from your customer, however. It will always be up to you to follow up your correspondence with a telephone call or a further letter.

Unconventional collection letters

The purpose of any business letter is to get a reaction. You do not have to write dazzling prose.

As mentioned earlier, it is a good idea to vary your letter cycles at irregular intervals. It is also possible to suspend these cycles from time to time, replacing them with non-standard collection letters.

It is also worth bearing in mind that in some collection circumstances standard letters will be inappropriate. In these situations, specially worded letters need to be skilfully put together. These letters will normally be to:

- ask for something
- provide an answer to an inquiry
- acknowledge a payment or dispute

You must assume your targeted reader is either busy or disinterested. He or she could even be hostile. Consequently, your letter must:

- always be civil, no matter how wrong you believe your customer to be
- be clear and to the point
- never be chatty, but factual
- separate each issue by a paragraph
- not be more than one page in length

To get past a secretary you must use phrases in your letter like: "As we discussed last week" and "You asked me to write".

It is essential that your letter be correctly addressed, i.e., name, title and department, to ensure that your designated reader actually receives it.

Let's imagine a typical day for the recipient of your letter. This person is probably very busy, perhaps unsettled by some incident or a problem with a member of their staff. When you letter arrives, they will have to take their mind off these troubles and concentrate their attention on your letter. So, you should make sure that the letter gets to the point quickly. Make sure that it also has a beginning, middle, and an end. For instance:

- it should begin with a reference to its purpose
- you should intensify your wording from polite to resolute
- it should end with a clear request or demand

Non-standard collection letters that could be used from time-to-time to temporarily replace a letter cycle or for other predicaments are suggested below.

There has been regular trading between us for nearly three years, so we are concerned that you have not reacted to our previous requests for the amounts overdue, namely £422.12.

Your remittance of the above sum is now required by return of post.

We have not received payment for the September account of £422.12, which became overdue a week ago.

Please pay this sum by the 14th of October 20XX, or tell us if you are having difficulty paying this sum.

We respectfully remind you that our credit terms are 30 days from the date of our invoice. On this premise, your account shows an overdue balance of £422.12. Your payment by return post is requested.

A reply paid envelope is enclosed for your assistance.

Thank you for the payment of £302.12 received today. This sum has been credited to your account. However, our reminders notified you that the sum necessary to clear your overdue account was £422.12. Your remittance was therefore short by £110.00.

Please forward this sum by return of post.

A self addressed stamped addressed envelope is enclosed for your use.

Our last statement indicated an overdue amount of £422.12.

Please arrange for immediate payment of this sum in full. Alternatively, let me know your reason for withholding payment.

Re: OVERDUE ACCOUNT - £422.12.

You have failed to reply to our previous demands for payment of the above debt.

Being unaware of any disputes, your account has now been submitted to CCS Collections, as mentioned in our previous letter. Any fees we are charged for their services will be added to your account.

Or fax to a finance director:

Dear Sir

FINAL DEMAND for £422.12.

Despite numerous reminders, we regret to find that the above sum remains unpaid.

We have stopped further deliveries to your company until this sum has been paid and until satisfactory arrangements are in hand for payment of future deliveries. This order effects your order number ABC 456, dated the 9th of November 20XX.

Our next step will be to instruct our lawyers to request leave from The Registrar of the (Any Town) County Court to apply for a county court order to enforce payment with costs. No further referral will be made to you.

To ensure reinstatement of deliveries and to avoid the action indicated, your cheque is required by return post.

Finally, at the time of posting any letters to your customers, you must decide upon a follow-up date if no reply is received. This may be in three or four days time, or perhaps a week to ten days. Always refer to the letter by its reference, date, and summary of contents when following-up letters that have been ignored.

Before chasing up any letters, check the days' cash intake to confirm payment wasn't received that morning. Look up the customer's history and contact record to see if someone other than yourself has taken a call in your absence, or if any disputes have been registered. This action will avoid wasted calls and needlessly upsetting a customer.

If you are fortunate enough to employ both sales and credit personnel, you should encourage them to work in unison. Representatives from each department could perhaps visit a customer together to sort out any misunderstandings, or to arrange for payment. Such a visit will instil into your customers' minds your combined efforts to be of service.

Making sure you get paid

6

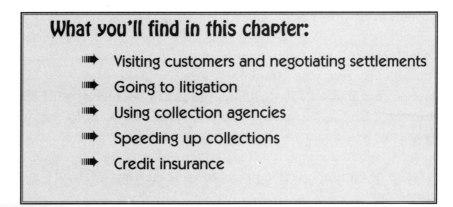

Chapter 6

Making sure
you get paid

What you'll find in this chapter:

- ⮕ Visiting customers and negotiating settlements
- ⮕ Going to litigation
- ⮕ Using collection agencies
- ⮕ Speeding up collections
- ⮕ Credit insurance

Guard against non-payment by maintaining accurate customer history and contact records. Having intimate details of your customer's organisation, and being on first name terms with all contacts will make it easier to negotiate, should a customer get into temporary financial difficulties.

This openness, together with your historical records, will bring any setback to light. The sooner any troubles are dealt with, the better it will be for all concerned. When a customer fails to pay, unless there are good relationships between you, it is impossible to tell whether they are unable to pay or whether they can pay but will not. Unless you have specific knowledge about your customer, do not assume the situation is calamitous from the outset.

Visiting customers and negotiating settlement

For most of us, there comes a point in our lives when we become financially stretched. Sometimes this occurs due to factors completely beyond our control. When a customer finds himself in the same predicament, he may want to pay you but he knows he cannot. You will need to discuss these problems with your customer frankly and preferably face to face.

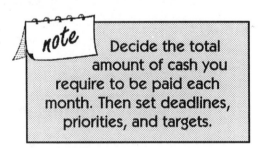

note Decide the total amount of cash you require to be paid each month. Then set deadlines, priorities, and targets.

One reason a customer might not be able to pay you could be because he has had a large customer 'go bust'. Suddenly he is faced with a hitch in the cash flow forecasts. Obviously, he will want to stay in business, and that may well mean you cannot be paid on time. In these situations, it is far better to negotiate a planned settlement of your account than to take the drastic step of cutting off all supplies to your customer.

Such an action could leave you in exactly the same position as your customer. Rather than trying to reach agreement on the telephone or by letter, it will be far better if you or your credit controller or manager do it face to face. Of course, you need not restrict these visits to times of stress. Reconciling the larger customers' accounts, or visiting them when they are first introduced, will help to understand how they operate.

Treat every customer, including the major accounts – the lifeblood of your business, with respect at all times. Don't ever forget the 80/20 ratio.

Primary accounts

The largest amounts due to you in any one period are probably owed by a small percentage of key accounts. Financially orientated visits will benefit both you and your customer. However, never simply turn up on their doorstep unannounced. Be professional, make an appointment. Above all else, be thoroughly prepared. This will mean:

- having the latest copies of their aged sales ledger
- taking a list of any outstanding disputes with you
- knowing what you wish to achieve from the meeting

Assuming it is possible, arrange your meeting for a time when it might be expedient to pick up a cheque, particularly if a large one is due.

The main objectives of customer visits are to foster better relationships, to increase sales, and to establish a balanced payment regime.

Unfortunately, some firms are so sales orientated that they take exception to anyone other than a salesman or woman visiting a customer's premises. This is a narrow-minded attitude that needs to be permanently discouraged. A well-planned visit will enable you to sort out any on-going problems that could be upsetting relationships between your company and the customer. Priority should be given to discretely analysing your customer's financial position and having a thorough discussion relating to:

- setting credit perimeters
- establishing a future payment schedule
- methods of handling their disputes

As soon as possible after returning to your office, a letter or report must be sent to your customer. This must highlight every single point discussed and any agreements reached and it must be done before memories have a chance to fade.

LETTER CONFIRMING PAYMENT BY INSTALMENTS

D W Computer Supplies
Anywhere Street,
Any Town 12ZZ 34YY.   November 28.20XX.

Dear

Re: Account No: WX 0098721.

Referring to my visit to your premises yesterday, I was sorry to learn of the cash flow difficulties you are currently experiencing. However, I was delighted to be in a position to offer assistance, as discussed.

It is confirmed the outstanding balance of your account, namely £1,758.34 will be paid by four monthly instalments. The first payment of £558.34 will be paid on January 1.20XX, followed by a further two instalments of £400 each on the first day of February, and March 20XX. A final payment of £400 will be made on April 1.20XX.

If any one of these instalments is not paid on the dates agreed in this letter, or if one cheque fails to be met on presentation to your bankers, the whole amount of the outstanding balance becomes due and payable.

It was further agreed to continue supplying you subject to any order not exceeding £950 in any calendar month, providing payment is received strictly in accordance with our trading terms in addition to the terms mentioned above. Any orders received from you in access of £950 will only be accepted on a 'COD' basis.

Yours sincerely

Proprietor/Credit controller/Manager.

Arranging for time to pay

Given that your visit had been purely to discuss helping a customer over a short term financial difficulty where it was agreed to amortise their overdue account whilst continuing to supply them, your letter confirming an arrangement allowing them to pay by instalments should comply with the sample shown earlier.

> **TIP** Some of the very largest firms, such as Ford, Shell etc, provide their suppliers with guidelines of their payment procedures. Follow them and you will be paid quickly.

The inclusion of the bold paragraph in the previous sample is extremely important. Without it, you could only sue for the missing payment, or wait until the agreement had expired, if your customer missed even one payment. By inserting this paragraph, you can sue for the full balance outstanding if your customer reneged on a single payment.

Going to litigation

note Litigation should only be used as a last resort, when every other collection method has been exhausted. The only exception is the situation concerning those customers who can pay, but will not.

When taking the agonising decision whether or not to sue a customer, the following must be considered:

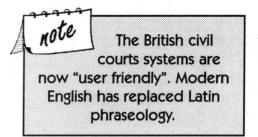

> *note* The British civil courts systems are now "user friendly". Modern English has replaced Latin phraseology.

- Can the debtor afford to pay, but will not?
- Is the customer unable to pay?
- Does the customer have adequate assets to meet the total debt plus costs?
- Are there any unresolved disputes preventing the customer from paying?

To discover the answers to these questions, look to the customer profile built up in their history and contact records. For those firms who have neglected to maintain these basic customer records, the services of a credit reference agency can be obtained to provide a 'Pre-sue Report'. These reports will:

- identify your debtor, i.e. sole trader, limited company, etc.
- provide head and/or registered office address
- list names and addresses of subsidiaries, or indicate if part of a group
- give details of bank and building society accounts
- list details of any assets
- state details of prior court judgement and orders

If your searches reveal the debt is really uncollectible, write it off as soon as you can and learn by your experience.

Taking a little time to obtain the above information will prevent wasting time chasing an insolvent debtor and avoid endless frustration. Knowing the correct identity of your debtor will avoid interruption to the serving of documents.

The system for recovering debts via legal proceedings is now cheaper, faster, and more straightforward than ever before. It is possible to pursue claims against a customer without using a solicitor, thereby avoiding throwing 'good money after bad'.

Remove bad or doubtful debts from your sales ledger before legal action or writing off a debt. Any account deemed uncollectible must be moved to a suspense account. This permits a true picture of your receivables to be reported each month and will quantify your cash flow forecasts. Make sure you don't forget those suspense accounts, however. They should be reviewed periodically and reported upon.

Sending a delinquent debtor a letter before issuing a summons giving them a final opportunity to pay is not a legal requirement. However, the court will need to ensure itself you have used every conceivable method to obtain payment prior to a summons being served. A final letter or notice will provide all the proof they will need. Anyway, you never know - your debtor may settle on receipt of your final letter!

Warning signs to observe

It is possible to detect signs of a probable bad debt. Analysing your customer's accounts ought to become second nature. Checking your aged sales ledger against individual accounts and inspecting their history and contact reports will direct your attention to potential dangers. Signs alerting you to likely insolvent customers could be:

- payments becoming slow or unpredictable
- cheques beginning to be returned unpaid
- delays in publishing annual accounts
- payment patterns altering from cheques to cash

Any one or more of the above changes can be a signal of a pending bad debt. Tighter controls must be imposed on any customer displaying these signs. A good customer is easy to spot. They're usually professionally managed and respond to your efforts to improve customer service.

Other signs of potential bad debt to watch out for are:

- loss of market share
- constant changes in management and staff
- financial gearing level exceed the norm
- premises that need refurbishing
- equipment that requires replacing

Danger signs like these can only be detected through regular customer contact and visits.

Using collection agencies

A third party debt collection service can be a boon to the small business, if used correctly. Their advantage lies in the way they operate, which is usually on a no collection, no fee basis. Having no contractual commitments, the agency works for as long as you require them. With no up-front charges, you know before the collection service commences work exactly what the cost to you will be.

TIP Before employing a debt collection agency, visit their offices and discuss the varying types of services they offer. Give them your instructions only when you feel comfortable working with them.

The use of an agency can be extremely cost effective. Their involvement instils in your debtor the seriousness of your intentions. Therefore, it can eliminate wasted costs of blind court action. Furthermore, if a customer has 'gone away' most agencies provide excellent tracing services.

Speeding up collections

Having said all that, there is no need to issue a summons or employ a collection firm to recover a debt. You can take a short cut and by-pass the whole system, providing your debtor owes you £750 or more. All you need to do is issue a notice under section 122(f) of the Insolvency Act 1986.

These statutory demands can be served on all types of debtors, companies, partnerships, and sole traders. Section 122(f) of the above Act permits a company to be wound-up if it is unable to pay its debts as they become due. To define proof, section 123(e) of the Act states clearly,

CAUTION Unless you understand what you are doing, never threaten or issue a statutory demand. Even then, only do it if you are prepared to go all the way.

'A company is deemed to be unable to pay it's debts as they fall due by forwarding a final notice to the company's registered office, giving it seven days to pay the account in full'.

This is sufficient proof in court, if your customer has failed to pay within the seven days. The same rule applies to partnerships and sole traders. The forms required to issue a statutory demand, after you have sent the 'Final Notice', are obtainable from any law stationers and have easy to follow instructions.

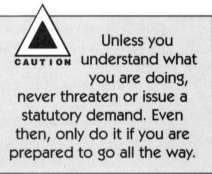

note The courts frown upon anyone using statutory demands without the intention to follow through with winding up proceedings.

If you decide to serve the demand yourself you will need to keep a note of:

- the time the statutory demand was served
- the address at which it was served
- the name of director, manager or other person to whom the demand was given

You will need to keep a note of this information because you'll be asked to swear an 'Affidavit of Service'.

Serving a statutory demand can have its advantages, particularly if your customer is solvent and only delaying payment to improve his or her own cash flow. Once they receive the demand, they will instantly pay up, because:

- they will not wish to be wound up
- they'll be afraid other suppliers will think they have financial problems
- it will upset their bankers

Unfortunately, while these instruments can be effective, they do have their down side. For example:

- winding-up costs are substantial and not always recoverable
- your customer's secured debts will have priority over your debt
- your debt will end up among a long list of unsecured creditors

Statutory demands have their uses, but they should never be abused. If it is your serious intention to take this route, it is advisable to seek legal advice. This is why the full methods for issuing a statutory demand have been omitted. Knowing both the advantages and the disadvantages will help you to decide on the best course of action suited to you.

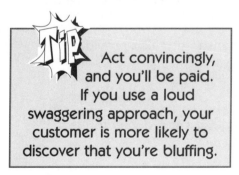

Act convincingly, and you'll be paid. If you use a loud swaggering approach, your customer is more likely to discover that you're bluffing.

Credit insurance

There is a well-developed credit insurance industry waiting to assist businesses experiencing loss due to uncontrollable events. Its underwriting skills rely on credit risk analysts and not actuaries as in the general insurance market.

The very first commercial credit insurer was Trade Indemnity Co. Ltd., registered in the last eight months of World War I. In fact, they are still trading today as a plc. It was not until the end of the World War II, however, that trade credit insurance really began to develop.

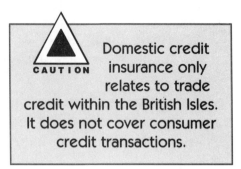

CAUTION Domestic credit insurance only relates to trade credit within the British Isles. It does not cover consumer credit transactions.

note

The aim of credit insurance is to compensate within a pre-set period of time that proportion of money lost due to the insolvency of a customer when goods have been supplied and delivered on trade credit terms.

Is credit insurance necessary?

You might be saying to yourself at this point, 'I'm operating within orthodox methods of credit management, so losses due to bad debts ought to be minimal. So why do I need to insure?'

note

Invoice factors and discounters also provide insurance cover via non-recourse deals, but at a price - you'll lose control of your sales ledger.

Apart from protecting you against the sudden loss of cash flow, credit insurance also provide:

- credit intelligence
- disciplined credit management
- access to additional financial resources at reduced terms
- self assurance and peace of mind

If there were still doubt in your mind, remember that throughout the process of manufacture and delivery, your products would be insured for loss due to damage or theft. Until you have received payment, the contract between buyer and seller is not complete. So, taking precautions against not being paid begins to make sense, don't you agree?

Consider the domino effect

Receivables represent a large investment in your business. Providing on-going credit assumes you expect to be paid before or on the due date. Assessing credit risk, whilst going along way to preventing bad debts, is not infallible.

> ⚠ **CAUTION** Credit insurers do not guarantee payment of a debt on its due date. They compensate in the event of insolvency or retarded default by a debtor.

They compensate in the event of insolvency or retarded default by a debtor.

Returning to the 80/20 ratio discussed earlier, suppose you had one large customer and the amount they owed represented 50% of your receivables. Disastrously, they have gone out of business. Not only would this situation make you insolvent, the effect on your cash flow would be serious enough to effect payment to your suppliers. In turn, they would be unable to pay their suppliers and so on. Now we have the domino effect, where any number of businesses may go under. Credit insurance can protect you and your suppliers from this type of catastrophe.

Principles of credit insurance

Cover up to 90% of the outstanding debt can be provided, but you are strongly advised to confirm this figure with your insurer or credit insurance broker, as the percentage of cover does differ widely between insurers. Trade credit insurance does not relate to either loans or overdrafts.

Credit insurers do provide help in setting credit limits on your customers. They are also indispensable when seeking market research intelligence. In domestic trade, sales to the following organisations are generally excluded from cover:

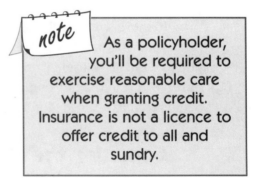

note As a policyholder, you'll be required to exercise reasonable care when granting credit. Insurance is not a licence to offer credit to all and sundry.

- local government
- national government departments
- any remaining nationalised industry
- associated or subsidiary companies
- misrepresentation and fraudulent claims

Payment is guaranteed in respect of an unpaid debt due to insolvency or protracted default.

Protracted default explained

DEFINITION

This means an insured debt is not paid for between 90 to 180 days after the period of credit has lapsed, or after the due date of postponement, had credit been extended. Proof of your debt and details of loss must be submitted to the insurer with all claims.

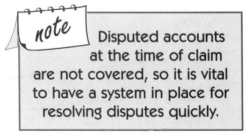

note Disputed accounts at the time of claim are not covered, so it is vital to have a system in place for resolving disputes quickly.

The length of time it takes to be reimbursed differs enormously between insurers. You must take into account these differing time scales when assessing which insurer to use.

note Credit insurance premiums are a budgeted amount to safeguard you against an unbudgeted expense.

The exception to the rule

Certain claims are excluded from the time-scales mentioned earlier. For example, when a customer has become insolvent, payment is immediate. As far as your insurer is concerned, the insolvency takes place when any of the events mentioned below occur:

- Your customer is adjudged bankrupt.
- Your customer enters into a voluntary arrangement with his creditors.
- An order is made by the court to wind your debtor up.
- An insolvency practitioner has been appointed in accordance with the Insolvency Act 1986.
- The debenture holders, or other creditors of your debtor company, appoint an administration receiver.

Types of policy

note

Insurance cover is available to any business that offers their customers trade credit, irrespective of the size of your business. It can be as flexible as you want; for instance, you may have insurance protection for any of the following:

- the whole of your sales ledger
- key customers only cover
- specific accounts – i.e. just one major customer

Premiums are calculated for each policy. The cost of cover depends on the extent of risk you wish to protect. Credit insurance referred to in this section relates only to the home market. The special requirements of exporters are covered in the next chapter.

Collecting overseas debts

7

Chapter 7

Collecting
overseas debts

What you'll find in this chapter:

⟶ Documents you must use

⟶ Export credit and finance

⟶ Methods of payment

⟶ Export credit insurance

Of course, the documentation and the way you will be paid when dealing with overseas debts is going to be different, but that shouldn't stop you from selling your goods and services abroad.

One of the fundamental pitfalls you'll encounter is the difficulty of resolving disputes over extended distances. Additionally, there are language problems to contend with. You'll have to learn to expect delays in payment for far longer than you experience at home.

However, do not be put off, help is only a 'phone call away. Because your trading terms will differ with each country you sell into, it's vital to ensure you are using the correct documentation. All orders must be confirmed in writing; to reduce the number of disputes you must state:

> Credit risk in an overseas market is not merely restricted to your customers. You must take into account unstable currencies and volatile governments when exporting.
>
> CAUTION

- the exact terms of payment
- the penalties for late payment
- an increase cost clause should commodity prices rise between order and delivery
- who is responsible for changes in currency exchange rates - buyer or seller
- when ownership of goods changes hands

Making business decisions in respect of exporting requires reliable marketing and financial intelligence. You can obtain such information from the following sources:

- Chambers of Commerce
- UK government departments
- credit insurers and factors
- bank reports
- trade attaches at foreign embassies

Two things you cannot afford to overlook when doing overseas business: using the correct methods of payment currently available and ensuring the sale does not contravene the laws of the importing country. Enhancing customer relationships by removing any foreseeable cause for complaint is always well worth the effort.

> TIP
>
> Make sure the right terms, conditions, and prices are quoted in all sales literature, to avoid problems arising.

Stating within your conditions of sale how any dispute will be dealt with, and imposing time limits, will help you to get paid, in part at least, should a query arise. It is also advisable to confirm the course of action open to your buyer if agreement over a dispute cannot be reached between you. One such option is arbitration by the International Chamber of Commerce.

Documentation you must use

The rules that define your obligations as an exporter and those of the importer must be clearly understood. Identifying the point where your liabilities end and your customer's begin can be seen in the chart displaying the most common definitions used in exporting.

Pre-stipulated delivery terms decide who is responsible for insuring the shipment, and when ownership of the products change hands. In the chart which follows, the term FAS means you are responsible for the consignment of the goods up to the time they reach the dockside. At which point the buyer has ownership and liability.

In some instances, the carrier can be held responsible for insurance during the time the goods are in his keeping. EXW means your customer is responsible for the cargo immediately it leaves your premises.

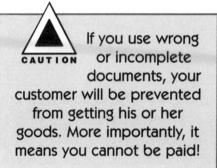

If you use wrong or incomplete documents, your customer will be prevented from getting his or her goods. More importantly, it means you cannot be paid!

EXPORTING TERMS AND ABBREVIATIONS

by sea

- Free alongside ship   FAS
- Free onboard   FOB
- Cost insurance, and freight   CIF
- cost, and freight   C&F or CFR
- Ex. ship   EXS
- Ex. quay   EXQ

all forms of transportation

- Ex. works   EXW
- Freight paid to + (name destination)   DCP
- Free carrier + (name destination)   FRC
- Freight and insurance paid to
  + (name destination)   CIP
- Delivered at frontier   DAF
- Delivered duty paid   DDP

The basic format of your invoices need not alter. But all prices must be based on above terms. They can be stated in either foreign currency or sterling and in any language. In addition to stating the details of your customer, the invoices are also required to display:

- weights and measurements
- packaging details
- customs declarations

Some countries require invoices to be certified by an independent body, such as a Chamber of Commerce, which can confirm they are correct in every detail. While this may delay shipping slightly, it does help you to get your goods through customs more quickly and thereby speed up settlement.

Transportation documents

Until the buyer can hand over the original documents to the carrier, he or she is unable to receive the goods. Freight forwarding agents will advise on the best transport and routes to use. They'll also arrange the movement of your goods and prepare the necessary documents for you.

In contrast to the simple despatch or delivery note at home, export transportation documents have three main functions, which are:

- to provide evidence of carriage contract
- to provide a receipt from the carrier for the goods
- to demonstrate title of goods in transit

note Check either with the importer's embassy, your local Chamber of Commerce, or a Business Link office to find out what documents are needed for the country you are exporting to.

Bills of lading

These can either be 'Received for shipment' or 'Shipped'. A thorough bill of lading covers a shipment from its point of departure to an inland overseas destination.

note Customs and excise should be consulted, in respect of duties and VAT regulations on exported goods.

A combined bill of lading covers the use of more than one form of transport. Goods shipped in containers that are shared with other goods use a groupage bill of lading. Other delivery documents would include:

- airways bills, which are receipts for goods shipped air cargo
- road or rail consignment notes
- post receipts, although these are not documents of title

Some of the most common forms of export certificates that you are likely to come across, and whose use is required by exporters are defined below:

➤ A certificate of origin

This is required in some countries who insist on a separate document, apart from the invoice, to confirm the origin of the goods being imported.

➤ Weight and health certificates

These simply confirm the goods were in good order and met the regulations of the importing country when they left your factory.

➤ Inspection certificates

These are used by a number of countries to confirm the quality and cost of the consignment.

➤ Export licences

These licences are mainly used to restrict goods capable of being used for military purposes. Food, drugs and livestock may also require certificates.

If in doubt about what can be sold overseas, always check with the Department of Trade and Industry, or your local Chamber of Commerce, prior to obtaining orders from abroad, and again before shipment.

Restrictions on other items can be imposed from time to time by differing countries, so keep abreast of the latest developments in newspapers and bank reports to avoid losses.

Export credit and finance

Financing the cost of exports must be given serious thought. The periods of credit granted to overseas customers would need to be extended. It may not be possible to finance these accounts from your current cash flow. Your bank's export and foreign currency departments can guide you on currency fluctuations and help you guard against risks.

Businessmen and women new to exporting are liable to offer 30 days credit terms, thinking of settlement as being within the same time frame as their home-based customers, but forgetting that an overseas buyer may be calculating the 30 days from receipt of the goods. Credit can be extended by other factors, such as:

- 2-3 days at the dockside
- 2-4 days in transit
- 2 days to clear customs
- 2 days to deliver
- 1-2 days before your overseas customer unpacks the shipment

Add to the above times the transfer of funds through the banking system, not forgetting any delay caused by the buyer being late in instructing his bankers or arranging finance. It is so easy for payment to actually take 2 to 3 months to reach you. These delays have to be financed; taking extended credit from your own suppliers is not the answer. The options are explained below.

Small exporter programmes

All major clearing banks in the UK operate small exporter finance schemes. They provide exporters with cash at the time of shipping, subject to the correct documents being submitted. Up to 100% of the invoice value can be advanced, less interest and a transaction fee.

note

Capital goods like vehicles, contractors plant and machine tools have special arrangements for finance and insurance via the Export Credit and Guarantee Department (ECGD).

The advance is without recourse as credit insurance is obligatory. Banks normally have block insurance cover arrangements which saves you from shopping around. Having insurance protection also means interest charges are lower.

Short term finance

Finance for a medium-sized business is available for up to 180 days. The arrangements are similar to the small exporter's programme, except the exporter is required to hold his own credit insurance policy. Taking advantage of this facility is easy. Shipping documents must be transmitted through the banking system to your customer in the normal manner.

> Although English is spoken extensively throughout the world, it pays to communicate with your buyers in their native tongue. It also greatly reduces the possibility of misunderstandings.

Once funds have been received, your account will be credited with the balance - after the bank has fully reimbursed itself and deducted its charges.

Export factoring

DEFINITION

Export factoring is based on the same principles as used in the home market. The main difference lies in the way disputes are handled. In export factoring, any invoices involved in a dispute are excluded from the factoring agreement and must be repurchased by the exporter.

Another advantage of export factoring lies in the fact that the sales ledger management will include the collection of overseas debt. This situation can be enhanced when the factor has overseas branches. Most factors offer a package of forward currency dealings to reduce the risk of losses through exchange rate movements.

Forfaiting

DEFINITION

Using either bills of exchange, promissory notes or a deferred letter of credit, which in layman terms are differing forms of IOUs, an exporter can sell or discount these bills to a forfaiting company. By doing this, the original benefactor of the note or bill, meaning you as exporter, forfeits his rights.

The difference between the bill's value and the discount price being the interest charges, there is nothing to stop you holding the bill to maturity which can vary from 90/180 days to two or three years. It is possible for the bill to pass from one forfaiting company to another; in these circumstances if your customer cannot pay, the final holder of the instrument has no recourse to you or any previous holder of the bill for payment.

Collections and methods of payment

Sales can be generated by using an export agent, who should also be involved with collections. Embassies and trade fairs are helpful when obtaining orders, but are of little use when collecting payment from abroad.

Appointing one or two main distributors in each country will eliminate the need for you to chase a number of smaller accounts. Distributors and agents need to be able to supply you with reliable economic reports on both markets and currency conditions.

Collecting debts from overseas

Ensuring that you get the money due to you from an overseas customer requires a methodical approach. The collection process must start before goods are dispatched. Its success will rely on your ability to follow every deal through from the initial order to final receipt. An exporter's resources must be devoted to preventing late payment on the same lines as at home. Legal action for overdue debts is both time-consuming and costly. Therefore, its use must be restricted only to extreme cases. The telephone and other collection techniques demonstrated in previous chapters can be adapted for use with export accounts. A check-list to help you in preventing late payments follows.

EXPORT COLLECTION CHECK-LIST

1. Acknowledge all orders and confirm payment terms
2. Establish credit status
3. Confirm currency regulation in country of delivery
4. Inquire if import/export licence required
5. Check letter of credit (if applicable)
6. Re-check if customer is credit worthy
7. Verify all export documentation is correct

if possible

a. appoint a local agent
b. send copies of all documents to that agent
c. chase banks for unpaid bills

avoid litigation - use debt collectors

Chasing for foreign payment

Sending letters, even using airmail, is a slow process and should be avoided. Using a courier may be faster and more reliable, but is an expensive alternative. If your transport contractor is obliging, or if have your own transport, a visit to a customer's office when you have another delivery close by is a good idea. However, the fastest and certainly the most efficient collecting tool is the 'fax' or E-mail. Demands and copy documents can be transmitted to your customer instantly.

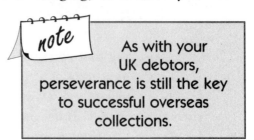

note

As with your UK debtors, perseverance is still the key to successful overseas collections.

Telephoning overseas

Telephoning overseas customers is well worth trying, provided you remember the time zones and you use your customer's native tongue whenever possible. Don't be put off by that last remark, English is very widely used. Avoid asking direct questions which can only be answered by a 'Yes'. In order to be polite, overseas buyers can't help saying it. Instead, you should preferably ask:

- have you paid our invoice for £.......?
- when did you remit the payment?
- how was it sent?
- why have you not paid?
- who did you complain to?
- when did you write or telephone?

Whether at home or overseas, you must press harder for the payment each time you chase your debtor. The methods used in Chapter 4 can easily be adapted for use on your overseas buyers.

note Contracts for overseas sales agents should contain a clause making collection of unpaid debts part of their duty.

Transferring money by mail takes too long, use your banker's electronic transfer systems bank whenever possible.

You might also find it useful to contact chambers of trade and local or international debt collection agents when you are trying to collect from customers abroad. If you use an export factor, the collect problem will be transferred from you to them. Personal visits can speed up collection and save you interest. The cost of travel can be offset if your visit coincides with a sales call or trade fair.

Preparation for all overseas visits must be thorough, since you cannot simply 'nip back' to the office to collect forgotten documents. You or your representative will need to take the following documentation and information along with you:

- name and position of contact
- copy invoices, and all export documentation
- full details of their account and how much they owe
- knowledge of the import countries currency regulations

Reasons for payment delays

Government actions or intervention can be another prime cause for delayed or non-payment. Moreover, it might not even be the importers' or exporters' governments that are causing the problems. Any country through which your goods need to travel could be to blame.

Among the problems you are likely to come across are:

- changes in law to prevent contract performance
- cancellation of an import licence
- acts of aggression or war or riots
- imposition of currency restrictions

Dunn & Bradstreet produce an excellent 'International Risk and Payment review' monthly. It highlights the main features of a large number of countries, including their current payment terms and transfer delays.

Unless you are an able negotiator, all payments will be received 'net of charges'. You must budget for this cost. All the international departments of major banks supply reports on specific countries.

Instruments of payment

Methods of payment can vary from the standard cheque used in home trading to documents or instruments not usually encountered outside the export trade. It is your responsibility as exporter to tell your overseas customers how and when the money due to you should be remitted.

A Bill of Exchange

The law relating to bills of exchange was set out in an act of parliament in 1882. This act deals with bills, cheques and promissory notes. In describing a bill of exchange, the act declares it to be:

'An unconditional order in writing by the drawer, to the drawee, and signed by the person giving it. The person to whom it is addressed is ordered to pay on demand, or at a fixed future date a certain sum of money to either the person or firm specified, or to bearer.'

As distinct from a cheque which is also described as a bill of exchange in the act, the drawer of a cheque is the creditor, and the drawee the debtor. The typical wording of a bill of exchange can be examined next.

BILL OF EXCHANGE

London

£9,250.00   29th September 20XX

AT 180 DAYS AFTER SIGHT OF THIS FIRST EXCHANGE (SECOND OF THE SAME TENOR AND DATE BEING UNPAID) PLEASE PAY TO OUR ORDER THE SUM OF STERLING POUNDS NINE THOUSAND TWO HUNDRED AND FIFTY POUNDS, ONLY. FOR VALUE RECEIVED.

To: <the drawee>   For and on behalf of

                                              D W COMPUTER SUPPLIES

                                              Proprietor.

Sight or term bills

DEFINITION

There are two types of bill in use; the sight draft, which is payable on 'sight' or 'demand', and the term bill, payable on a fixed future date, normally 90 but can be up to 180 days hence. Attaching a sight draft to an endorsed bill of lading, which is the delivery note transferring ownership of the goods, allows you to obtain payment before losing control of your products.

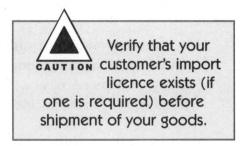

Verify that your customer's import licence exists (if one is required) before shipment of your goods.

Term bills, on the other hand, are negotiable instruments and can be discounted for cash during their life.

Obtaining a Bill of Exchange

As the exporter you will prepare a draft and send it either directly to or via a bank to your overseas customer for payment or acceptance. The draft is a standardised form supplied by banks setting out the details for:

- handling collection
- how to remit the proceeds of sale
- who pays the charges
- the point at which the goods change ownership

DEFINITION

Bills used for export purposes are generally referred to as documentary bills. They will have the export documentation attached, enabling you to control the release of goods via instructions to the bank.

Credit cards can, in certain situations, be an ideal instrument of payment. They certainly remove a lot of paperwork!

A non-documentary bill can be used where the customer's credit is beyond reproach, so if they can be avoided it is advisable to do so. It is also possible for bills of exchange to convey an interest clause.

Letters of credit

A letter of credit is a conditional authority to pay. It relies upon the performance of both parties and the correct documentation to enable payment to be made. Failure to cash letters of credit usually stem from the exporter's inefficiency due to:

- not keeping to the stated terms
- delays in shipment
- unresolved disputes
- incorrect forms used for the country of destination
- wrong shipping documents for instance, a bill of lading is used instead of an airways bill

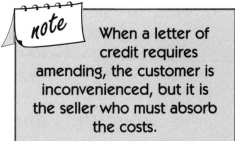

When a letter of credit requires amending, the customer is inconvenienced, but it is the seller who must absorb the costs.

Letters of credit become payable only after your customer's conditions have been met. In line with the contract of sale, your customer would instruct his bank to issue a letter of credit through a bank in the exporter's own country. This instrument would list all the documents required to transfer ownership and state the date of shipment. Immediately you present the documents to the advising bank, they will pay you. On receipt of the documents, the bank forwards them to your customer so that they can pick-up the goods on arrival.

Avoiding delays in payment

There are two good ways to avoid disputes arising. The first is to give precise instructions to your customer of your requirements, and the second is to agree in advance with their proposals.

Checking, on receipt, that the letter of credit is correct will side-step a letter of credit failing to be paid. The examination of a letter of credit should confirm that all documents are correct, that they have been received from the various departments of your organisation and that the dates for shipment and lodgement have been met.

Export credit insurance

In addition to protecting yourself against loss due to protracted default or insolvency, cover is also provided against political risk. The credit intelligence reports insurers provide can be invaluable to any budding exporter.

All credit policies offer suitable collateral for bank advances. Combined cover for both home and export markets is readily available.

For many years, the Export Credit & Guarantee Department (ECGD), a government department, led export insurance. Since privatisation of their short term insurance cover, ECGD specialises in providing insurance and guarantees for larger sales of capital goods and projects. Contracts for smaller consignments of consumer goods and raw materials are now in the hands of the private sector. The numbers of insurance companies providing cover continues to grow. There are now many foreign firms setting up offices in this country.

Premiums and cover

There are no limiting restrictions in respect of cover, unlike the domestic market. Indemnity is provided up to 100% of the debt, depending on whether or not the insurer cover can include or be negotiated for the following eventualities:

- loss of import or export licence
- kidnap and/or ransom
- non-delivery due to political interference

Premiums are based on individual policy requirements. Annual premiums are normally quoted, but it is possible to pay either quarterly or monthly by direct debit.

 CAUTION Various services on offer differ from insurer to insurer, so it's advisable to shop around to get the cover and service that's right for your business.

These extra services are available free of charge from insurers. While some insurers restrict use of these services by volume, others have no limitations. You can obtain cover for both developed and undeveloped countries, plus:

- on-going credit management and debt collection facilities
- country and/or currency risk appraisal
- credit opinion service
- provision of credit limits - this can be compulsory in some policies

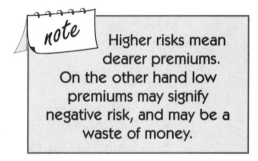

Higher risks mean dearer premiums. On the other hand low premiums may signify negative risk, and may be a waste of money.

When weighing up the cost of credit insurance, the level of risk should be the deciding factor.

Support services for the exporter

Government backed support is available for the larger exporters and those undertaking substantial overseas projects via it's Export Credit and Guarantee Department (ECGD). The support system offers you services that will:

- enable you to offer your customers finance packages where required
- provide cover against non-payment and help you if things go wrong

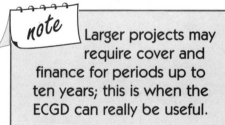

Larger projects may require cover and finance for periods up to ten years; this is when the ECGD can really be useful.

Besides providing export insurance cover against insolvency, default, war or civil disturbance, cover is also available in situations where countries run out of foreign exchange. This has happened in no less than 62 counties in the last 16 years. It sounds unbelievable, doesn't it?

ECGD also provide guarantees to UK banks offering overseas finance packages to your clients. They are able to use their vast banks of customer data to assess credit risk. If your customer is unknown to them, the ECGD will make enquiries through the normal channels, embassies, and consulates.

ECGD services are designed basically for the larger exporters and contractors. Smaller firms should contact their local Chambers of Commerce.

There are many other facilities offered by ECGD in addition to those stated above, these are:

- claims and recoveries
- lines of credit
- tender to contract cover
- forward exchange supplement
- protection prior to finance being arranged

Details of their full range of facilities are available to all new or established exporters. To contact them, see the Sources of Credit Information that follows this section.

Sources of Credit Information

Collection agencies

Commercial Collection Services,
797 London Road,
Thornton Heath, Surrey CR7 6YY.
Tel: 020 8665 4900
Fax: 020 8683 2283

Dunn and Bradstreet Ltd.,
Holmers Farm Way, High Wycombe,
Buckinghamshire HP12 4UL.
Tel: 01494 422000
Fax: 01494 422260
www.dnb.com

Credit reference agencies

Extel Financial Ltd,
Fitzroy House,
13-17 Epworth Street,
London EC2A 4DL.
Tel: 020 7251 3333
Fax: 020 7251 2725
www.info.ft.com

Dunn and Bradstreet Ltd,
Holmers Farm Way, High Wycombe,
Buckinghamshire HP12 4UL.
Tel: 01494 422000
Fax: 01494 422260
www.dnb.com

Experian Ltd,
Talbot House,
Talbot Street,
Nottingham NG1 5HF.
Tel: 01159 410888
Fax: 01159 344905
www.experian.com

Credit insurers

Export Credit and Guarantee Department (ECGD)
PO Box 2200, 2 Exchange Square,
London E14 9GS.
Tel: 020 7512 7000
Fax: 020 7512 7649
www.ecgd.gov.uk

Coface LBF,
15 Appold Street,
London EC2A 2DL.
Tel: 020 7325 7500
Fax: 020 7325 7699
www.cofacelbf.com

NCM Credit Insurance Ltd,
2 Harbour Drive, Capital Waterside,
Cardiff CF1 6TZ.
Tel: 01222 824000
Fax: 01222 824003
www.ncmgroup.com

Trade Indemnity plc,
1 Canada Square, London E14 5DX.
Tel: 020 7739 4311
Fax: 020 7860 2847
www.tradeindemnity.com

General business addresses

Association of British Chambers of Commerce (The),
Manning House, 22 Carlisle Place,
London SW1P 1JA.
Tel: 020 7565 2000
Fax: 020 7565 2049
www.britishchambers.org.uk

Department of Trade and Industry (Export Licensing Branch)
66-74 Victoria Street,
London SW1E 6SW.
Tel: 020 7215 8070
Fax: 020 7215 8564
www.dti.gov.uk

Registrar of Companies,
Companies House,
Crown Way, Cardiff CF4 3UZ.
Tel: 01222 388588
Fax: 01222 380900
www.companies-house.gov.uk

Associations

British International Freight Association,
Redfern House, Bromwells Lane,
Feltham, Middlesex TW13 7EP.
Tel: 020 8287 3525
www.bifa.org

Factors and Discounters Association,
18 Upper Grosvenor Street, London
W1X 9PB.
Tel: 020 7290 6938
Fax: 020 7290 6924
www.factors.org.uk

Index